'*The Launch Handbook* has go
and that message is: how to ge ssage right!
In this ground-breaking book Mal McCallion walks the talk with three decades of experience eruditely inked into one fantastic resource for all serious entrepreneurs. Whether you have an idea and need help realising it, or need pointers to get your marketing and sales right, this is the formula for your success!'

— **Dr Darren Stevens,** Founder of the 'Constructed Development Theory', entrepreneur and psychologist

'In *The Launch Handbook*, Mal McCallion clarifies the key areas of focus for your startup to be successful. The content is accessible with actionable tips and crystal-clear examples. This should be the first book you read if you're launching or relaunching a business in the 2020s.'

— **Sam Zawadzki,** Founder and CEO, Property Technology Ltd

'*The Launch Handbook* has what all entrepreneurs need – a structured approach to building their business from scratch. Working through the different "Elements" helps to clarify each and make sure that you're not missing anything. For those starting out, it's essential reading – and for those already in business, it's a great way of keeping the startup energy and direction going.'

— **Sarah Turner,** Founder and Executive Coach, Bloom People

'*The Launch Handbook* is the "business how to guide" for experienced professional and new business start-ups alike... What the handbook does for business owners like me is ensure we're always constantly analysing our business purpose and processes and taking that information to drive forward to refine our business... It emphasises that entrepreneurs are everywhere among us and we can all do what we set out to achieve. Of course, having *The Launch Handbook* makes it a lot less painful! It's a great read with lots of gems to utilise to help move your business forward.'

— **Ashley Mckella,** Founder and Director, Agent Hub Ltd

'*The Launch Handbook* is an actionable guide – much like a manual – ideal for business owners looking to bring a sense of rhythm to their business plan. The author confidently stewards you through a formulaic sequence of executable activities that both gets you to market and prepares you for growth. What I liked most about *The Launch*

Handbook was how I could work through each of the modules with my team, making it an altogether more inclusive experience.'

— **Stephen Willard,** Founder and CEO, Emblaze

'*The Launch Handbook* is a really structured, helpful way of thinking about launching or relaunching a business. Whether you're in the profit or non-profit sector, the ability to be able to focus in on individual "Elements" of business really helps to shape growth in a measured and achievable way. A must for anyone looking to build and grow in the 2020s.'

— **Colleen Amos OBE,** Founder and CEO, Amos Bursary

The Launch Handbook

Rethink

First published in Great Britain in 2021 by
Rethink Press (www.rethinkpress.com)

To Haroon

The Launch Handbook

How to turn
your great idea
into a profitable
business

Mal McCallion

Let's get growing! :)

Mal

Contents

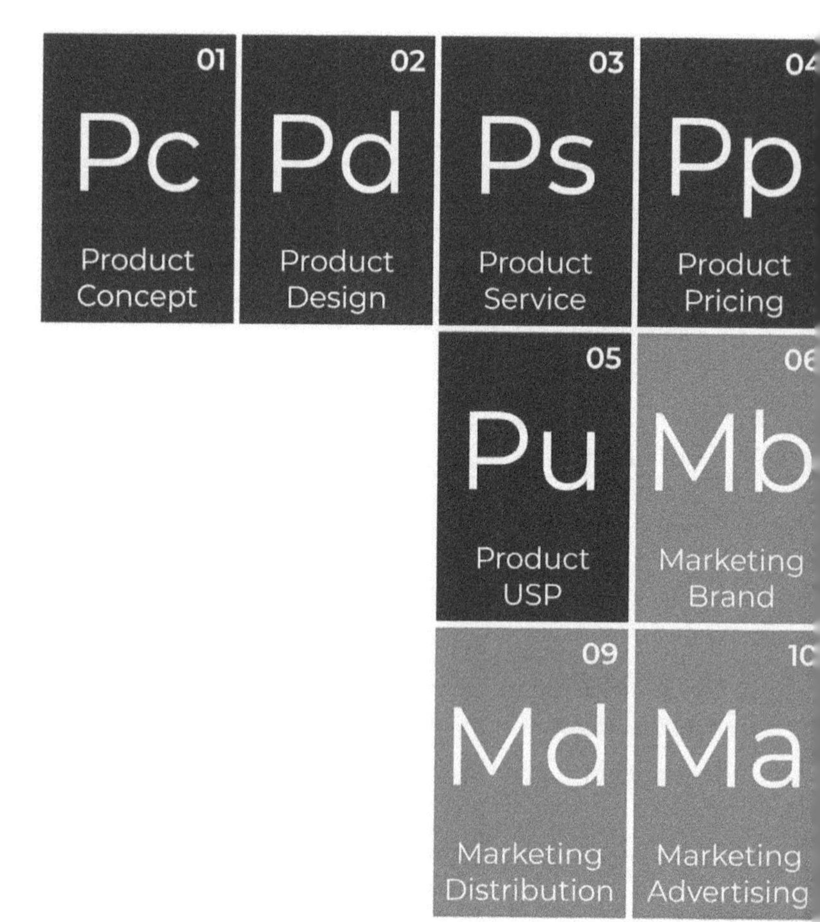

01
Pc
Product
Concept
02
Pd
Product
Design
03
Ps
Product
Service
Pp
Product
Pricing
05
Pu
Product
USP
Mb
Marketing
Brand
09
Md
Marketing
Distribution
Ma
Marketing
Advertising

INTRODUCTION
GROWTH EXECUTION

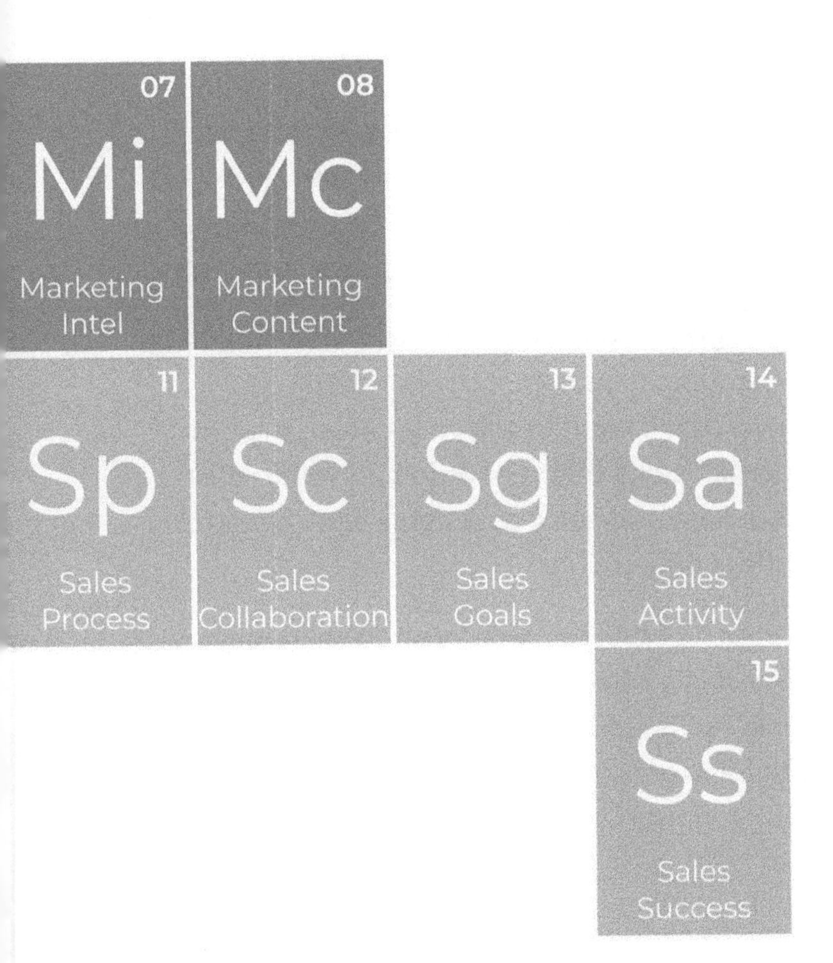

formulation: what is the Growth Execution Formula?

The coronavirus pandemic of 2020 had a dramatic effect on the number of new small- and medium-sized enterprises (SMEs) being created. In the UK alone, from June (when the initial unprecedented lockdown ended) to December there were 38% more limited companies incorporated than in the same period for 2019.[1]

In adversity, it is often said the brave come into their own. The courage shown by these new entrepreneurs was underpinned by three key factors, coming together uniquely at this moment in history:

1. **Furlough** – if you had a mind to consider setting up a new business before the pandemic, but perhaps didn't want to risk your career, the brutal economic reality might have forced you to dust off your idea and see it as a viable alternative to relentless uncertainty.

At the same time, never before had there been such an availability of 'soft landings' for those who wished to take the risk to set up on their own. Many who might have been made redundant were, instead, put on 'furlough', meaning that at least 80% of their

[1] Companies House, July to December 2020, http://download.companieshouse.gov.uk/en_output.html

salaries were paid, even though they could not work. Although not available to everyone, the ability to use this cash to speculate on a new venture provided enough of a cushion to enough people, that the leap of faith facing all new entrepreneurs became less of a yawning chasm to cross.

2. **Thinking time** – whether you were on furlough or working full-time at home, you sure had a lot more time to consider whether your current employment was really where you wanted to continue spending your dwindling life resources. The death statistics were starkly revealed each and every day, and the 'degrees of separation' between you and someone who had succumbed to COVID lowered rapidly – rarely can the Stoic exhortation *memento mori* ('remember death') have been more straightforward.

We're all going to die in the end. Should there be, many thought, a bit more planning and control involved in what the remaining years contain? And what about this idea to launch my own business? Can I really get it out?

3. **Technology** – never, ever, has there been a better time in history to become an entrepreneur. Not only are we blessed by platforms that enable us to communicate with potential customers effortlessly, we're also plugged in to vast networks of individual expertise to call upon, share documents

with and borrow passwords from – and all without leaving our bedrooms.

And so, as night follows day, enterprising individuals look up from their position in someone else's world and plan for a place in their own.

Whatever your reason for deciding to launch your own business, here's where the problems start: 60% of businesses fail in the first three years.[2] No amount of energy, allied as it may be to a great business idea, can make up for a lack of structured thinking around what's needed to execute on growth.

That's where *The Launch Handbook* comes in. Across thirty years in startup and scale-up businesses, I've been lucky enough to have been part of some great launch stories, including Zoopla and Primelocation.com. In that time – and across dozens of successful, and some unsuccessful, businesses – I've been obsessed by what it is that makes some organisations grow, while others flounder.

The result is the three-discipline, fifteen-element Growth Execution Formula. This structured approach

---

[2] Rob May, 'Start-ups across the UK are going bust – they need more careful management for our economy to boom', *The Telegraph* (24 January 2019), https://www.telegraph.co.uk/politics/2019/01/24/start-ups-across-uk-going-bust-need-careful-management-economy

to launching and growing your business gives immediate as well as medium- and long-term guidance on what your business needs to grow – fast.

Desmond Tutu once said that the only way to eat an elephant is one bite at a time. Launching a business can feel like just such an undertaking. Let *The Launch Handbook* guide you through each mouthful, and advise you on the order in which to set about consuming them, too.

segmentation: what does each discipline cover in *The Launch Handbook*?

In the **Product** discipline, you'll discover all the elements to create the perfect solution to your future customers' problems.

In **Marketing**, you'll learn how to articulate your story and build value for the people you are here to serve.

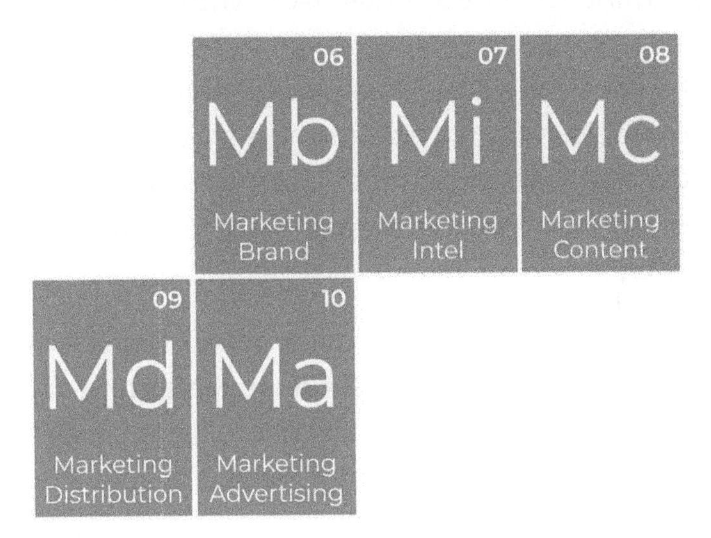

In **Sales**, you'll find out how to turn the leads that you've generated into delighted, profitable, paying clients.

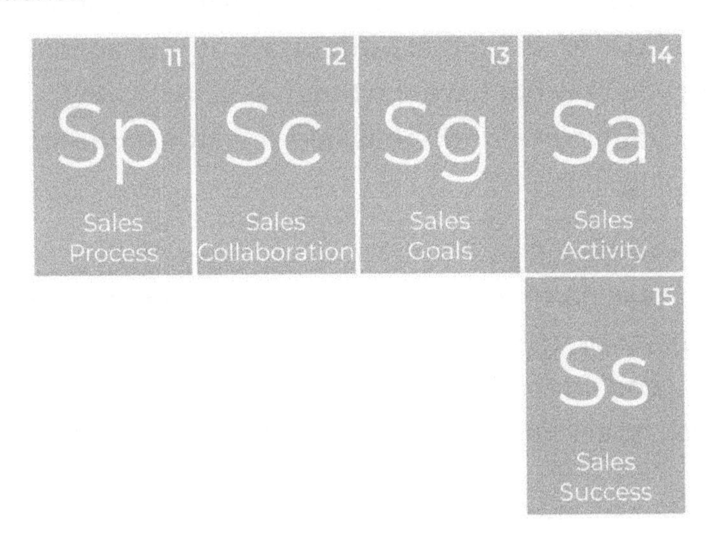

navigation: how to use *The Launch Handbook*

The Launch Handbook has been written with the freshly minted entrepreneur in mind. This is not a linear, one-size-fits-all trudge through an immutable system – it's a formula that's geared to the needs of any founder looking to fast track their launch, while avoiding as many bear traps as possible.

To that end, you can find a quick overview of each of the three key disciplines – **Product**, **Marketing** and **Sales** – on the next pages and get to know a little about the five elements within each of them.

Once you've checked them out, you might want to start from Element 01 (E01), Product:**Concept**, and go all the way through to E15, Sales:**Success**. That way, you can be certain to complete the learnings around everything that's important as you launch. But you may not have the time – and that's why *The Launch Handbook* has been created to reward 'dipping', too.

For example, if you're about to sign up with a potential partner, head over to Sales:**Collaboration** (E12) and learn how to maximise the credibility, data and advice partners can provide you with. If you haven't quite worked out a suitable name yet –

or you're wondering whether consistent fonts are important – then get across to Marketing:**Brand** (E06). If you don't know how much to charge at launch, Product:**Pricing** (E04) is the place to go. Or if social media seems like it's going to devour you, spend some time in Marketing:**Distribution** (E09).

However you choose to use *The Launch Handbook*, there is only one thing that you must do – and that's cover off E01, Product:**Concept**. This is, without doubt, the most important element of the whole Growth Execution Formula, and without it, you will waste an inordinate amount of time in unproductive work. You need to know that more than anything else.

This is it, then. You ready?

Let's get growing!

formula elements

The most important element in your business – its 'Why?'

How does your product get clients from 'vague interest' to 'voluntary advocacy'?

Who is your product really for? What are their service expectations?

Incorrect pricing can ruin a launch. Where's your sweet spot?

If you're not unique, you're not going to grow as you should.

Consistency and coherence ensure that clients believe your promises.

Unless and until you know what your customers do, your growth will suffer.

Committed, regular, consistent messaging reinforces identity.

So many channels for distributing your content – which is best for you?

Paying for advertising is a huge play; first, you need to understand what works.

How does your process perform in converting sales? Is it fit for purpose?

Who's talking to your customers already? Partner up and grow faster.

Measure it, manage it – without clear goals, your growth will suffer.

Now it's time for the hard work. Who's making sales happen? How?

Congrats – you made it. But what's next? How do you scale up?

resources

Use these other resources to help you on your launch journey:

- **Growth Execution Group:** Full, free launch support – search 'growth execution' on Facebook

- **Growth Execution Tips:** Insights for your launch every weekday – sign-up at www.growtion.co/tips

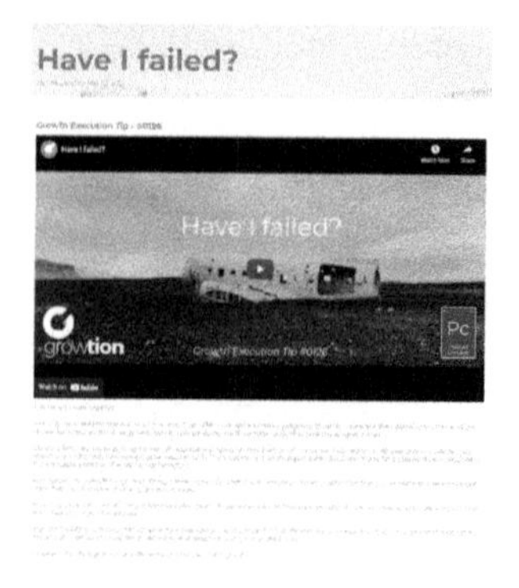

- **Growth Execution Podcast:** Search 'growth execution' for launch stories on your favourite podcast feed

- **Growth Execution Academy:** Full 'Launch Program' – see www.growtion.co/academy

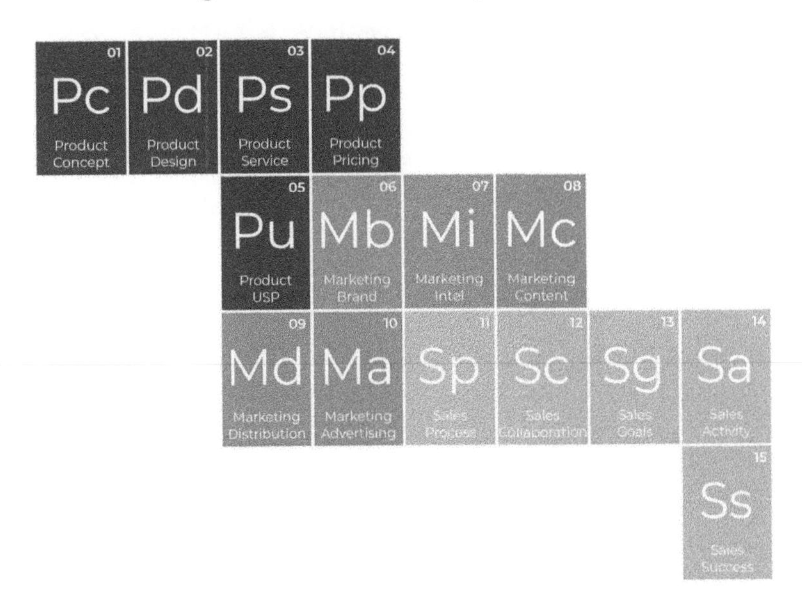

DISCIPLINE ONE
PRODUCT

introduction

There are three critical things to remember as you work through the five elements of the Product discipline:

1. 'Product' is not just something that you can touch. A product can be anything you expend energy on that you then exchange for money or barter for another product. Your product is whatever is of value that you are seeking to exchange for money.

Whenever we mention 'Product', we're always talking about services, too. Whatever you're going to swap for revenue, that's what Product is. This includes (but is not limited to) apps, Apples and apples; CEOs, SEO and essays; trousers, transfers and translators.

Be clear that Product is not just a thing; it is the exchange of value, the idea or object that you are going to transact upon.

2. Product is the most important of the three key disciplines. No disrespect to Marketing and Sales – they're important parts of your business and its launch, too, of course – but without a product, you've got nothing to market. Without a product, you've got nothing to sell.

That's why Product is the first discipline, that's why it's the most important, and that's why I encourage you to spend as much time as you need here. Make sure that your product is right for you, it is going to fit the market correctly, you understand your audience and know who the people are you're here to serve, you've got the pricing right, and you know what your unique selling proposition (USP) and the design of the product are.

We will cover all of these elements of Product within this discipline, but just keep remembering – this is critical. There is no more important area you're going to need to focus upon to get the launch of your product or service firing successfully.

3. Your priority is to get to product market fit (PMF). PMF is where the market is absolutely ready for what it is that you are looking to deliver. And – there is no gentle way to impart this news – it is *very* difficult to achieve. If there is one thing that defeats the majority of startups, it's this – they cannot get the market to appreciate what they're putting out there.

The good news? If it were easy, everybody would be doing it. That's why you and your product have this opportunity right here, right now – because others have looked at this idea, perhaps even tried it, and given up. Of course, that may be because there is genuinely no need for what it is that you're thinking of doing.

That may sound like devastating news, but it's not. If your idea is right but, currently, your chosen delivery mechanism (product) is not, you'll find that out, as others may have before you. They gave up. You will not.

The Launch Handbook is here to take you on step-by-step iterations, so that you produce something that the market genuinely wants. There are, I'm afraid, so many disheartening tales about people launching products, taking them out to market, and nobody caring. Armed with curiosity and resilience, you will ensure this is not to be your fate. Every knockback is the market asking for more information, more iterations.

But the first thing your future customers, and you, have to know – intimately – is why you're doing this.

Shall we find out?

The most important element in your business – its *why*.

ELEMENT 01

Product:**Concept**

defini**tion**

Human beings have a real problem – they can't get past the question 'Why?' until they either:

- Categorically believe the answer they have been given; or
- Have created a satisfactory answer around it for themselves.

Until you find a way to truthfully, consistently and coherently articulate why it is that your business exists, the majority of people simply will not care enough to bother to find out. As a result, you will not win their business.

This is why Product:**Concept** is so important – and why it is the first element in the Growth Execution Formula. It filters down into each and every other element, too. In Sales:**Collaboration** (E12), for example, you won't be able to find the best partner to add credibility, data and advice to your sales effort unless you share their ethics and outlook.

That requires you to know your – as well as their – *why*. Marketing:**Content** (E08) is the repetition of your *why* on an ever-expanding scale. You had better be consistent, or you cannot build the all-important trust upon which your launch success depends. Product:**Service** (E03) needs to know your *why* so that it can identify the people you are here to serve and ensure that your product is built with them in mind.

And so it goes on, through Product:**Pricing** (E04), Marketing:**Brand** (E06), Sales:**Goals** (E13) and the rest. You need to know *why* this thing is important to you, so that your *why* can inform how you execute upon each element.

That's the theoretical basis for this element. But how do you find out, practically, what your Product:**Concept** is? Well, the good news is that you don't need to search far – its core is inside you.

There is a reason *why* you're even considering launching this venture, isn't there? Perhaps it's an issue that you have direct experience of – you've genuinely felt the pain of the problem and have a distinctive and, you're pretty sure, successful way to solve it that others aren't delivering yet. Or perhaps you've looked on from afar at a situation that you know – really know – is not being addressed in the right way. You've done some research and you're confident that it's a market and an opportunity you can fix.

To gain the clarity needed to identify your true Product:**Concept**, you need to answer just one question:

'Why am I solving this problem?'

There is genuinely no shortcut to getting the answer to this. It requires a considerable level of self-reflection and self-awareness. All successful entrepreneurs – those who achieve true significance for their businesses – have these qualities in spades.

You, too, need a full awareness of your internal drivers to achieve in the task that you have set out to conquer. This enables a flexibility which a *why* provides – one which a *how* never can.

Consider what happens when you approach a market in one way that proves to be wrong. If you are only focusing on solving the problem via a particular method – the *how* – then you've got nowhere to go. This means the end of the project, the finality of failure.

Instead, if you come at the challenge from a position of knowing *why* you're approaching it, then the possibilities remain pretty significant. We'll come on to iterations and the search for product market fit (PMF) in the next element, Product:**Design** (E02), but for now, just consider how different the future might have been for Blockbuster Video had it considered its Product:**Concept** to be 'providing the best in-home entertainment' to its customers, rather than being hung-up on the profits that it made from VHS and DVD rental. What might the future of Kodak have been had it continued to emphasise 'capturing memories' (the *why*) rather than 'selling photographic film' (the *how*)? The apocryphal tale with Kodak is that the company actually developed the digital camera in the 1970s but hid the technology so that it didn't impact on its core business model. I think it's safe to say that in the end, it did. And it always does.

Be clear about your own *why* rather than any particular *how*. The latter comes later. Even if the *how* doesn't need iterating immediately and you hit the bullseye with your tactical game straight away, there's always a possibility that you'll need to be nimble in the future. And that, dear Founder, is when you'll be really grateful for the clarity your *why* brings you.

To home in on your *why*, let's you look at the two distinct sides to the question in **Product:Concept** – **you** and the **problem**.

You

Ahh, wonderful, complicated, resourceful, ambitious, dedicated you. You've got some stuff to do, things to fix. But what's really behind that urge? Is it as simple as a transactional opportunity to carve out something that might make you a bit of cash?

Rarely, I've found, is this the case. There is something deeper running in most entrepreneurs, something that it is useful to draw out. If you haven't done a lot of mindfulness work, there are some great apps around these days to guide you, including Calm and Headpsace. In particular, I have found MindFi to be really useful both for myself and those I mentor.

Alongside these apps, another way of getting closer to your real *why* is to create a Personal Board. This is a group of individuals – I've found five is a good number – who cover off your weak points, so if you are particularly risk-averse, you might want a risk-taker to offer you an alternative point of view. If you're terrible with money, you might want someone to guide you a little on what *really* constitutes a sensible launch budget.

My five weak points are that I'm too much of a worrier, a financier, a disciplinarian, a coach and an innovator. What would you go for? If you need help and advice – and even perhaps a name or two – head on over to the growthexecution group on Facebook. It's free and is there to support you right the way through this launch journey of yours.

Problem

Articulating the problem is the other half of the Product:**Concept** process. What exactly is happening and why does it need fixing? What else is out there already, solving it in some way? And why is that not enough? What's being left out of the solution that you know – really know – needs sorting out? And by you, and you alone?

This brings us neatly on to our ac**tion** for this element – the one thing that you need to do next before you move on. But before we look at that, how about a Growth Execution Tip or two?

GROWTH EXECUTION TIP #0114 - WHY PURPOSE AFFECTS EVERYTHING

When you know why you're doing something, things become so much more straightforward.

Want to hire someone? Check that they share your purpose. Looking for an investor? A shared purpose means more support (and probably more cash, too). What about customers? Once they understand why you're solving this problem, the people for whom it is important will flock to you.

From potential business partners, to brand colours, to marketing content, to how hard you push in sales – everything starts, as the great Simon Sinek says, with *why*.[3] So get to know yours.

Ask yourself, 'Why am I solving this problem?' and dig it out. If it won't come immediately, or doesn't feel true, keep on asking *why*?

Far too few SME businesses, at launch or afterwards, articulate their purpose – and that makes it much harder to achieve. Simply, you'll end up with the wrong team aiming at the wrong targets with the wrong product. That's not a recipe for success.

Take time now to work on your purpose. Embrace it. Articulate it. Then you'll find that others will spontaneously self-select to join you in the pursuit – and it won't feel as far away as it does without them.

GROWTH EXECUTION TIP #0105 – INSIDE THE MIND OF YOUR CUSTOMER

'What will others say?' This is the daunting question that guides a lot – too much, one might argue – of human decision making.

Brilliantly described in Seth Godin's *This is Marketing*,[4] the nature of the human tribe has always been to identify hierarchy and maximise our place within it to further our own individual interests. This necessarily means judging and being judged on the decisions we make, on what we spend time on, and what we acquire.

---

[3] S Sinek, *Start With Why: How great leaders inspire everyone to take action* (Penguin, 2011)

[4] S Godin, *This is Marketing: You can't be seen until you learn to see* (Portfolio Penguin, 2018)

So far, so Neanderthal. But we humans have been busy since, developing 'justification'. Our newest part of the brain, the neocortex, is awesome at explaining why what we are doing right now just happens to be the instinctive thing that we want to do anyway.

As a growth executor, you need to make sure that your product is playing to your tribe's intrinsic desires. Does it help them to achieve more for others to see? Can it demonstrably win them more friends and influence? Do your reviews tell the next cohort, without any doubt, what the previous one has won in no small part as a result of your hard work?

Daunting as it may sound, 'What will the others say?' is a key driver of the behaviour of your next customers. Make sure that the answer to that question is hugely positive and you will reap considerable rewards as a result.

Tens of thousands of years of evolution have made it so.

ac**tion:** interrogate the problem

Is the problem genuine?

If you have yet to ask yourself this question, you need to sit down, get a pen and a sheet of paper and write, free-form, about what the problem really is and how it affects those who struggle with it. (You may close this handbook once you've read to the end of this paragraph.) Is it really something that causes enough of a reaction in those who experience it for them to demand a new solution?

Or is there enough out there to let them muddle through without much thought – and certainly without having to spend the kind of money that you're thinking of charging (we'll check those assumptions in Product:**Pricing** (E04))?

Whichever it is, you need to know – and you need a convincing case to explain not just to yourself, but to any significant others with an interest in what you are about to take on.

Who has the problem?

A by-product of answering this is that you start the detailed thinking about the people you are here to serve, something we'll deal with in detail in Product:**Service** (EO3).

For now, it will suffice to consider some broad brushstrokes around what their desires are and why they're in the position to need your help anyway. In particular, consider the *why* for them, too. Are they all driven by a particular need?

For simplicity, I've found that it's useful to broadly adopt the idea that people only ever act from two drivers, fear and greed.

Is it fear or greed that's driving people to continue to suffer with this problem? And once you've isolated the answer to that, can you build up a picture of the personalities of the people who need your product?

Then, be honest – are these people the kind that you want to spend the next five years helping out?

How big is the problem?

You know that it's a genuine problem now and have some idea of those who suffer from it – some of whom may still be unaware of their pain. But are there enough of them? Is the problem really and truly that important to solve?

This is a good time to do some quantitative research on the numbers of people operating in a particular way, or who are members of particular groups or work in particular industries. It can make or break your idea.

resolu**tion**

Product:**Concept** is, without doubt, the most important of all of the Growth Execution Elements – and the one that you need to know inside out before you step further.

'Why are you solving this problem?'

What's so important about it that you simply can't stop solving it? That gives you the confidence to know, regardless of how difficult it might get in the short and medium term, you're going to keep on ploughing through? Because it's not in the rush of new creation, in the thrill of building something new for people that have yet to realise what you're about to do for them, that success lies. It's in the ability to deal with the lows, the obstacles to progress, the moments when you wonder if, truly, this can ever be worth it.

Those moments will come. So, you'd better have a damn strong reason to continue.

You'd better have a damn strong **Product:Concept**.

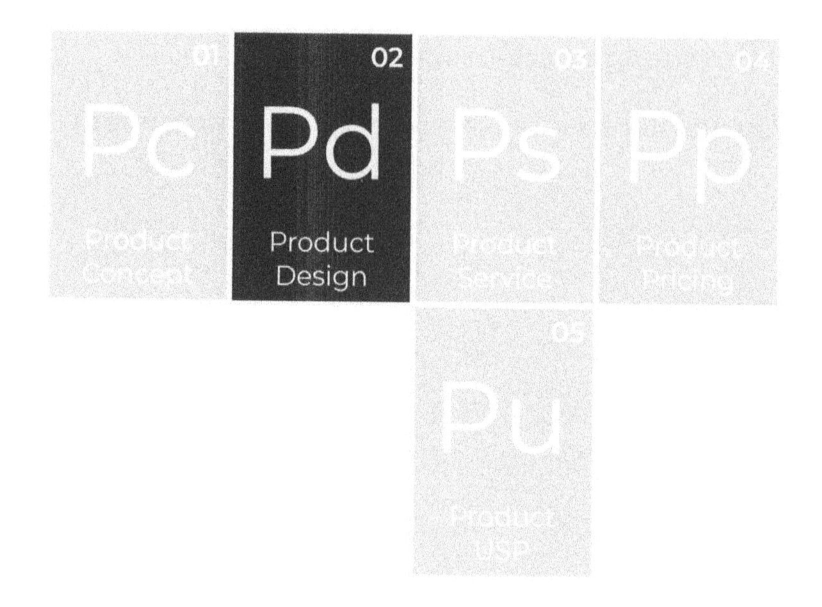

How does your product get clients from 'vague interest' to 'voluntary advocacy'?

ELEMENT 02

Product:**Design**

defini**tion**

The chances are high that you have some idea of what to do here. Product:**Design** is the manifestation of your solution to the problem that you articulated in Product:**Concept** (E01). It is the challenge that you have set yourself to satisfy a need, then take it on to advocacy via delight.

Why do you need to go that far? Why isn't it good enough to be good enough? The answer lies in the interconnectedness of our world today. In these times, you are creating a business when the art of conversation has developed to the point that one 140-character microblog, one grammatically poor sentence, one hashtagged word can ripple around the world at lightning speed.

You can complain about it, celebrate it or wilfully ignore it, but this is where you live – the global playground, in which everyone's talking about everyone else and the latest stuff gets instantaneous word-of-mouth reviews. You can try to game the system, tee-up some visible positive feedback and seek to build momentum as a result. But there's one thing that you can't fake – the experience your target audience actually has with your product once they get their hands on it.

And woe betide those who are found to have been blagging it at this point. 'You can fool some people some of the time, but you can't fool all people all of the time,' as Abraham Lincoln didn't say. The blaggers will feel the backlash – highly visible or spread underground through online groups and/or disinterested algorithms – for years to come.

Make no mistake – you need to back up your product promises with a Product:**Design** that delivers exactly upon them. Advocacy has to be the intended outcome – not only to avoid the negativity of poor feedback, but also to save a huge amount of cash on Marketing:**Advertising** (E10) in the medium and long term.

How do you start on the journey to advocacy? The first thing you've got to do is to get something out there that your initial audience can have a play around with. This is called a minimum viable product (MVP).

MVP was popularised by Eric Ries in his ground-breaking book *The Lean Startup*,[5] which I

[5] E Ries, *The Lean Startup: How constant innovation creates radically successful businesses* (Portfolio Penguin, 2011)

recommend highly at every opportunity. For now, I'll try to summarise the idea as succinctly as possible.

Basically, you don't have the time or the resources to over-engineer your product to the point that you think it's perfect. Worse, your view of what's perfect compared with that of your target audience is likely to be all manner of degrees off. The world is littered with products that entrepreneurs thought were the absolute bee's knees, sometimes backed by considerable investment and output before they realised that beyond a faithful few, no one needed what they had created. It was, in short, a solution looking for a problem.

This is not the fate that I wish to befall you. And to that end, you are going to have to get busy. Here, more than anywhere else, you'll require real dedication and resilience.

Your MVP needs to be the lightest, least-costly attempt to solve Product:**Concept**'s problem that you can muster. I cannot emphasise enough just how important it is to *not* spend more time or money on this than you have to. Fancy flourishes are out, hardy hacks are in.

It has to work, but it does not have to feel as beautiful as you are going to make it – not yet. This is where the feedback-loop starts – where the action and reaction of you and your target market work symbiotically together to iterate and reframe the solution until it starts to appeal to more and more and more people.

There are many reasons why this is the best way to develop a product. For me, the most important one is product market fit (PMF). You can spend a long time working on something alone, imagining the amazing reaction to your creation, then when you do open the door and present it to the world be greeted with a gigantic collective shrug.

'It's OK,' is worse as a response to your gift to the globe than genuine hatred of it. At least with the latter, you've generated some impact, some passion. It's received feedback that you can use – the hater may be right or wrong, but at a minimum, you now have something to work with. And that's the beauty of momentum – it feeds off itself and builds to a higher-level of attainment than anything done purely as a solo pursuit.

Alongside the critical fact that your MVP has to solve the problem that you laid out in **Product:Concept** (E01), there are a couple of other things to consider as you build it out, then iterate from the feedback you get.

Usability

This will naturally flow from the reactions you get to the MVP and its future iterations, but it's so critical that it requires flagging here.

Your Product:**Design** has to be user-friendly. If you miss out some niceties from the MVP – and you should – then don't forget to introduce them later. The idea of 'friction' is as real in product use as it is in physics – the slower you make it for your audience to reach the prize, to achieve balm for their painfully problematic wound, the less likely they are to get there. Every single point of friction – every time they have to make a choice, click a button, read some text, scroll up or down – is a point where some will exit the process.

This is bad for you.

At one particular tech startup I was part of that went on to be worth many millions, we obsessed about 'three clicks'. Everything had to be designed so that a customer could get where they needed to go – find the solution to their problem – within three clicks or fewer of a mouse, three taps or fewer of a screen, otherwise we were failing them. As a discipline, it was really helpful, as it gave clarity to a process that might otherwise have become flabby and unwieldly.

This is the kind of thinking that you need around usability. Even if the MVP and iterations one to five don't specifically focus on the delight of the customer's journey, your product needs to get there later. Otherwise, you'll be putting people through a machine that they will rebel against in the end.

Scalability

The ability to improve flaws, once you're making some money, is always there. But there is never any harm in thinking about how they might come into play as early as possible.

Your job is not to fashion one product, and then walk around high-fiving everyone at your brilliance. You have to execute on growth. That means you need to understand what it takes to create – and market and sell – a vast array of these things. The sooner you consider scalability in your iterations, the better.

At its core, **Product:Design** is all about flexibility. You'll have to make changes on the fly, hear some pretty awful things about how ugly your 'baby' is, and remain utterly faithful to your end goal.

GROWTH EXECUTION TIP #0207 - TOUGH LOVE

Have you ever had to sit there while someone gave you some really harsh, honest feedback?

I'm not talking the constructive criticism that you have from your manager when you first start out in employment, or the word that your parents have with you about your school report card. Just one true, glaring, open, genuine response to something that you've done.

It's cathartic, like an ice-cold shower. It washes through everything, shaking your certainties and forcing - not asking - you to take a good, hard look at what it is that you've been doing with your life to this point.

If you have someone that you can ask for this kind of feedback right now, make some time today. It's more difficult, you might think, in these atomised times when we spend so much of our lives on our screens. Or is it?

Perhaps this distance actually makes it easier for someone to gift you that openness across a video call. Perhaps, if you were physically together, you or they would bottle it and just slide into the usual platitudes that cover most of our true thoughts and feelings.

Steel yourself and find some honest feedback on what you're doing. Capture it today. You probably know it already but hearing it from someone else might just spur you to do the right thing to fix it.

GROWTH EXECUTION TIP #0214 - HOW DO I STOP MY BUSINESS GOING UNDER?

Almost every successful business has its survival story – the time it nearly went under.

At Primelocation, within a year of launch, we had to start charging our shareholder customers a monthly subscription fee to stay afloat and keep their investment in play. It was a radical pivot – no one else, even market-leader Rightmove, was charging agents for listings in 2001. But we survived and eventually sold for £48m four years later.

Zoopla pivoted from being a private sales website to an agent subscription service in 2008 – it was sold ten years later for £2.2b.

The moral of these stories is: don't be too proud to change. Circumstances are so different now and there's no shame in fixing your business model so that it fits the market as it is, not as you wish it to be.

The way to save your business is to be honest with yourself and every stakeholder about the challenges it faces and get creative about the options. If you need to radically pivot, then you need to do it fast so that you've got more cash for the next phase.

Do it now. You could be looking back at your best move in a few years' time.

action: launch your MVP

Invite initial cohort. This is predicated on the belief that you have created the aforementioned MVP, based on the advice shared so far in this element. If that's proving difficult, get some help from the Growth Execution Group on Facebook (search 'growth execution' on Facebook) – it's free and there are loads of great entrepreneurs there who have collectively done this hundreds of times.

Once you're getting close to being ready, it's time to identify your first cohort of testers for the product. This is not a small undertaking, so take care to find the right people. You need to find a community – it could be an online group, forum, club, cult – wherein a number of your target audience interacts. Answer some questions. Show expertise. Then ask a handful of them to help you out in return for some free goodness. You'll be surprised how keen many will be to fiddle around with your new prototype, provided you pitch it correctly.

Install metrics. The boring bit – you have to measure the responses to the MVP, otherwise how are you going to know what to iterate from/to?

Before MVP-launch day, make sure you know what it is that you're testing for. What do you need the most urgent answers on? Is it purely factual, the flow through a website? If so, make sure that your analytical platforms are geared up for the task at each possible interface. Or is it more of an emotional response that you're looking to test, what people think and feel about your MVP? If so, you need to get surveys or polls either into the process via links or scripted out for a manual questionnaire.

But be wary – that famous quote of Henry Ford's always leaps to my mind when I'm surveying potential targets for brand-new product features: 'If I had asked people what they wanted, they would have said faster horses.'

Launch MVP. You've got the measures and the measured in place – now it's time to get the MVP out there. This is a genuinely big moment, so it's worth acknowledging the emotional impact it could have. Assuming that you've been true to your **Product:Concept** (E01), this thing has part of you in it, and that means it's not an entirely objective rollout.

Give yourself some time to relax around this. Meditate, if that's your thing (and most successful entrepreneurs do). This is the start of something huge – and it's got you all over it.

resolu**tion**

Congratulations! You're on your way.

Every journey starts with a single step, and that's what Product:**Design** is here to get you to take – quickly. The more you mess around, the more you ruminate, the less chance there is that you're going to actually crack on. So, don't procrastinate.

Get that MVP out as soon as you possibly can, and then listen to the feedback. There's your momentum, right there, because you'll be hearing people genuinely interacting and reacting to what you've produced. And you will have a duty, an expectation – whether as a result of your desire to be true to your Product:**Concept** or true to your audience (which is essentially the same drive) – to keep building, iterating, and then checking that you're getting closer.

This is how great products are designed.

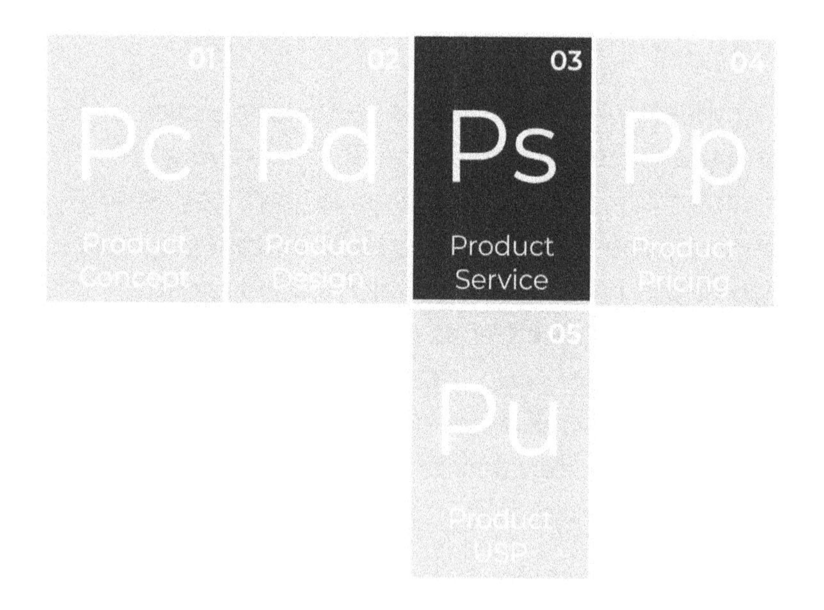

Who is your product really for? What are their service expectations?

ELEMENT 03

Product:**Service**

defini**tion**

We are so used to the word 'service' – the service sector, services on the motorway, service-oriented products – that it's easy to forget what it really means. As we focus on it in this element, it's worth just taking a quick detour into its definition, as that is where the key to this aspect of your product lies.

'Service' is, according to the *Oxford Dictionary of English*,[6] 'The action of helping or doing work for someone.' And what is a product if not a direct intention to achieve this?

It's important to focus on the idea of 'someone'. In your mind's eye, there needs to be a figure or group of people that you want to inspire to get involved with what you're doing. And it is that person or group that we are concerned with here in Product:**Service**.

Who is it that you are here to serve?

---

6 *Oxford Dictionary of English* (Oxford University Press, third edition 2010)

Perhaps you'd like to start with those you know will be interested. These could be close to you, perhaps family, friends or acquaintances who have expressed enthusiasm for what you want to do. That's a niche, for sure – but is it one that can be scaled up to a significant business in time? It's unlikely, unless you are phenomenally popular, have an eyebrow-raisingly large family group or have astonishing networking skills. On the basis that these situations and skills are not available to most of us, in *The Launch Handbook,* we're going to have to look further afield for a cohort that we can scale.

Let's go to the opposite extreme and consider the whole of the market. Can't we just go after everyone and see what happens? This is one of the key lessons that founders of young businesses often have to learn the hard way: if you spread your net too widely, you lose on multiple levels.

Product clarity. Your breadth of targeting means that the product has to do a lot of work to support multiple different customer types. Some might want a family product, others something that works for the singleton market. Still more may want couples in general, but another cohort wants the product to come in for single-sex couples only. The less specific you are in terms of who you're here to serve, the more trouble you are storing up – and costs you are pre-spending – in pursuit of people who are not really going to go all-in for what you are creating.

Marketing clarity. If it's bad enough having to have a broad product foundation that can service pretty much anyone, trying to communicate that breadth of offering to that breadth of potential customer base requires a Herculean effort. One of the key problems is that to create a platform for scalable and sustainable growth, you need to drive up inbound leads. This requires a subset of prospects to take it upon themselves to get in touch with you – and sadly, it is only those who really identify with what you're doing, believe what you believe, want to take your solution and make it theirs, who will do this. And that means creating something highly targeted for them, not something universal.

Sales clarity. You'll learn all about Sales:**Process** in E11. Suffice it to say at this point that you're trying to get as many people to progress down a funnel from prospect to customer as you can. Throwing the world in the top and hoping some of them stick is demanding a lot of your Sales resource – which is highly likely to be limited this early in your company's life. It's far better to be particularly choosy in your initial selection than to expend all of your energy (and cash) on people who are unlikely to convert into delighted advocates.

As you need to focus in on a niche, what niche should you choose? Guess where the answer to that little conundrum is? Right back at the start, in Product:**Concept** (E01). If you followed the instructions to complete that element first, you can just pull out the answer to the question 'Why am I solving this problem?' here. If you did not, then bad you! You're going to have to go back and do it now.

That answer to why you are solving a certain problem will guide you back to the problem. And it is only people who have this problem that you need to consider right now. If you find that the cohort you're seeking to serve here is too large, then ask yourself some additional questions about the target audience to help to slim it down to manageable levels. These can include whether they're in the prime or volume markets, their gender, age and life stage, their interests and their geographical location.

What you are doing via this segmentation of the market is starting to drill down into the minds of your potential clients. This takes a natural next step into creating genuine personas of them. These personas or avatars are sketches of the lives of each type of potential client for your product. They will have a number of different attributes that it's worth considering in detail.

Market quality. People in the luxury end of the market have different requirements to those at the volume end. Obviously, you will sell far fewer products to the top-end at a far higher price if – and only if – you are prepared to produce a level of quality in your product that you can keep consistent, allied with a Marketing:**Brand** (E06) that articulates its desirability to the audience effectively. At the volume end, this is less of a consideration, and so the Marketing:**Brand** needs to convey value rather than quality.

Gender. Those of a particular gender – or who choose to define themselves by neither – can have distinctive requirements in certain situations. Your product may appeal equally to all genders, or you may find that it can be more effectively targeted at one group rather than another.

Age and life stage. Whether we like it or not, our tastes change over time. Experience, physical development and simply not wanting to look like we're pretending to be seventeen can all have an impact on product choices. Inevitably, whether we have children or dependent older relatives, and whether or not we are single, can also be extremely relevant to what we buy.

Interests. Music, sport, art, TV shows, video games – there are any number of differing interests, and therefore differing avatars, that we can adopt.
It's more the combination of these that requires thought because, complex as we humans are, there is little that completely unites us. Again, this is where your Product:**Concept** helps significantly with ruling things in and out.

Geography. Localism is an increasing feature of our atomised world. There is a perceived desire to shop locally, yet our high streets have never been so bare. 'Belonging' in whatever tribe remains critical, though, and frequently geographical location can act as a surrogate for all manner of other belonging imperatives.

Beliefs. Religious or political – those conversations you never wish to have at dinner parties – are just a couple of the exciting, weird and downright worrying beliefs that your target audience may indulge in. Understanding how they tick can open your market up in ways that throwing Marketing:**Advertising** (E10) at a wall and hoping some sticks will not.

Now you've got more of an idea who the people are that you're here to serve, what's the best action to take to really get them into your launch sights? We'll have a look at that action in just a moment, after a couple more handy Growth Execution Tips.

GROWTH EXECUTION TIP #0307 - ARE YOU QUALITY OR QUANTITY?

One of my favourite truisms is that, as a customer, you can have a product which fulfils two of these attributes, but never all three: fast arrival, low cost, high quality. You can have it quickly and cheaply, but it won't be high quality. High quality and low cost may be available, but it won't arrive even remotely quickly. Or you can have high quality tomorrow, but it is going to cost you.

You have a similar choice to make as Founder of an SME providing products. Do you choose quality or low cost, ie quantity? (The third attribute, speed of arrival, is less important for the majority of people while you build.)

Quality comes with a price tag to match and will narrow your audience-base - but they are likely to appreciate that rarefied atmosphere and unique exclusive feel, and thus buy more. If you go for quantity, you can get away with things not always being perfect, but you'll flood a lot more out into the market and make more profit in pure volume terms.

What you need to do is to go back to the reason you're here - is it to serve as many people as possible, or to provide the best service possible? You can't do both equally - not with the resources you are likely to have at your disposal as an SME.

Is your focus to be quality or quantity? Pick your side and stick with it.

GROWTH EXECUTION TIP #0313 - DO YOU KNOW YOUR AUDIENCE? REALLY?

Easy one this, right? Every business owner knows their audience, or they wouldn't have one, would they?

But do they *really*?

You can get an audience and grow to a certain size with a basic level of knowledge about your customers, for sure; but you won't maximise growth unless you spend time thinking much more deeply about their behaviour, beliefs and needs. Creating avatars is a great way of doing this. Select up to three personas that your customers generally fit. Give them all names, then flesh out each by answering these three questions:

1. How do they behave?
2. What are their backgrounds and how have they shaped their beliefs?
3. What do they need to solve the particular problem I'm here to fix for them?

Spend a little time right now on clear thinking about who you are here to serve. Use it wisely, construct strong and identifiable avatars, and then get serving them with your product.

Then you can honestly say that you *really* understand them.

action: identify your niche

Who has the problem?

Armed with the responses to the questions from the previous few pages, you're in great shape to answer this one. But it's the combination of answers that is really critical in shaping your Product:**Service**.

If you were looking to solve the problem of people losing their spectacles, for example, a product for wealthy older women who like cruises will likely differ from one dedicated to dog-owning hikers based in the Scottish Highlands. Not only could you charge differently (see Product:**Pricing** [E04]), you might also consider what the technological intensity of the product needs to be. Would one group find it easier to adopt than the other?

Where is the problem most intense?

While this won't always be the decisive factor in your decision regarding who to target, often you'll find that those who feel the issue most keenly are those who are most willing to pay to relieve the pain.

This is where market knowledge is critical. Many people may be suffering in silence and not be willing to talk openly about their plight. Others may not even be aware that they have this problem and are just content to carry on solving it crudely through current means when it arises. To return to the spectacle-loss scenario, these people just accept that it's a 'fact of life' and go and buy another pair. It's only when the solution is presented to them that they see it as something to fix.

Psychology plays a huge part in whether people are going to take up the solution that you're offering. It's important that you understand the mental state of the potential buyers at the point of purchase so that you can further increase their buying frequency.

Are there enough of them?

A critical question, allied to the price that you're going to pull together in the next element, is Product:**Pricing** (E04). Clearly, if your target customers only number a few and you can't charge a lot, then you need to broaden your base. That means expanding the problem into another geography, gender, age or interest group, or another category of purchaser.

Alternatively, you may have too many target customers to serve them happily – and remember, they will all talk – so you'll need to increase the severity of your filter to rule more people out. Keep the niche as tight as you can – it will pay huge dividends in the rest of the build-up to launch.

resolu**tion**

We have spent much of this element inside the brain of your future customer. Understanding and being able to identify with them is an absolutely critical part of creating a product that is going to launch successfully, and then grow scalably.

The next time we meet your customer in detail will be during Marketing:**Intel** (E07), when we'll discover granularly where they hang out and how to approach them with your marketing messaging. In the meantime, you need to work out what they're going to pay you for all of this hard work.

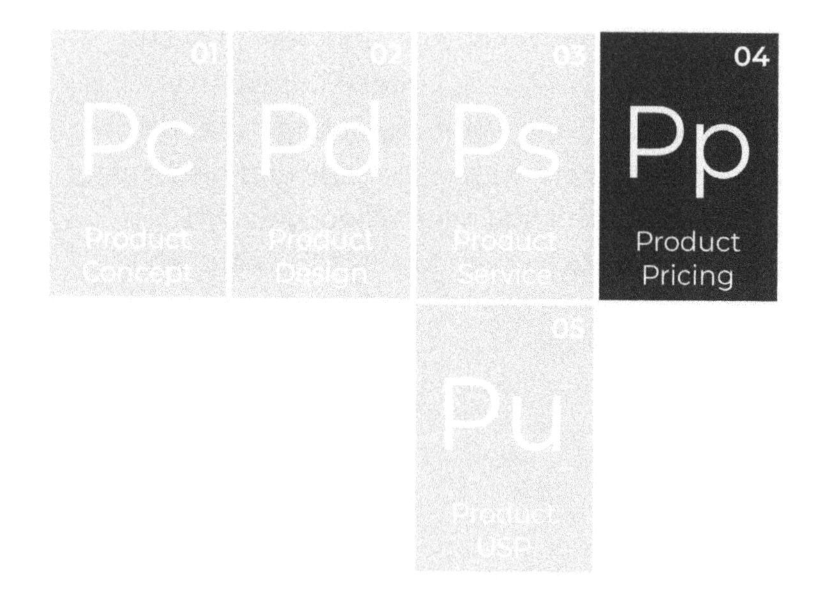

You've got to launch with the right pricing – where should it be?

ELEMENT 04

Product:**Pricing**

defini**tion**

Some of the most fun you can have with your launch is on Product:**Pricing**.

Getting this right is something that stretches even the most seasoned of entrepreneurs – and getting it wrong at launch can be a business hit that is incredibly difficult to recover from. So where do you start? The easiest thing to consider is where you want the price to be in three years' time. This is for three clear reasons.

1. **Mindset.** You have to assume that you're going to be in this game for that long. How does it feel? Are there worry lines creasing your forehead at this possibility?

Let's be real – this is not a get-rich-quick endeavour; the chances of that are incredibly slim. If, in the rarest of flukes, you manage to shin up the greasy pole in no time, congratulations to you. This mindset will keep you grounded and focused on getting to the next level – scale – even more quickly, too.

2. **Practicality.** Charging your long-term price at launch is pretty arrogant. You will have to have some really strong proof that what you're positioning the product as is true: a highly compelling proposition in a relatively competitor-free market and a strong marketing budget to articulate the value and gain trust quickly. That is a lot of work to justify something that you can change at a stroke.

3. **Trust-building.** Early adopters – those who quickly recognise your value proposition and want to be in from day one – like to see their faith rewarded. A super-low entry-point price is one way of sealing that informal contract. But without knowing how your product is going to escalate over time, you'll easily offend them if you discount even more for those who come in, say, Month Seven. This can have a hugely negative impact on your biggest fans – and as we'll see in Marketing and Sales, you're going to need those guys.

If three years hence is where to focus, how on earth do you arrive at that future price? This is where you can divorce the oppressive competitive environment that you are launching into from the optimistic world that you'll have created in three years' time. Let's get future-telling.

What are the costs of producing your product? If you've gone through Product:**Design** (E02), you'll have a pretty good idea – even though you're likely to still be in the iteration phase, and will probably remain there for some time to come, of what it takes to make what you do. You'll be well beyond the startup costs by Year Three, so can make a really honest assessment of the variable costs of production. Think labour and parts as well as distribution and any setup costs.

I always add in 15% for Marketing costs by that stage, plus a consideration for profit margin. This will depend on your industry, but (incredibly broadly) should be 10% for something physical and 40% for something online.

This is all very general, of course, and is intended for guidance only. Every single business in every single industry has to make some really smart decisions based on its own experience, so if this feels crazy to you, then it's not going to work. However, they are numbers that can succeed, so if you are genuinely interested in how to get Product:**Pricing** right and you're coming without preconceptions, then this is as good a place to start as any.

The unit price you come to is what you want to pop into a thirty-six-month spreadsheet as being the charge in Months Twenty-five to Thirty-six inclusive. Now you can work back from there. In Year Two – Months Thirteen to Twenty-four inclusive – you'll want to charge 75% of that. You can introduce some additional urgency drivers (UDs) in the form of setup fee discounts, free upgrades etc as you go through this section – more on that in a second.

Year One – Months One to Twelve inclusive – is the time that you need to use Product:**Pricing** to build trust. Coming in at anything less than 50% of your Year Three target price for the whole year will give you a huge credibility gap to bridge as the months unwind.

The recommendation is to have the 'headline' price in this year at 50% of Year Three, with a view to flexing a little in the startup Months One to Six, where you might go down to 40%. But please don't fall into the trap of going lower. Having a launch price of 10% doesn't say 'bargain'; it says, 'this is not worth the 100% price and I'm really just chancing my arm.' Focus on presenting dignity and a plan in your Product:**Pricing**. These are absolutely central to creating a sustainable and credible company.

Now you have an idea of what you need to charge for your product – congratulations, it's a big moment. But this is strategic and long term. What of the short-term need to drive business in now?

This is where your UDs come in. There are three and, in these early stages, they can be used in rotation.

UD1 – Discounts

We've already discussed the escalator that decreases the strategic discount on Year Three Product:**Pricing** over time. The UD discount is very different – it's a tactical discount, monthly on rotation, that encourages selected prospects to take a dive into what you have to offer quickly. I'm sure we've all experienced how Black Friday discounts can make us commit to a purchase that we might otherwise not have made – well, here's your version of that.

It doesn't have to be massive – 20% off your current rack rate – but it needs to be time-limited and upfront. If you're in Month Four and this is your chosen UD, you're going to want to show that this discount is a *further* 20% off the 50% discount on usual price.

UD2 – Free setup/delivery

There is an upfront cost to what you produce that you can remove to create purchase urgency. Generally – although not always – a business-to-business (B2B) product might have a setup fee and a business-to-consumer (B2C) product might have a delivery charge. If your product doesn't at present, create one. It doesn't have to be large and it doesn't have to relate to too much, in terms of the work that the task really requires to complete. What it does have to be is there, visibly, and charged on purchases outside of the month that you decide this is the UD to deploy.

Again, the onus is on you to be upfront and open about this during the UD period as well as either side of it. People are very precious about Product:**Pricing** and can feel terribly hard done by if they think they've been hoodwinked into paying a higher price than they would if they had just waited a few days more. Bring your faithful customers with you and they'll bring others along, too.

UD3 – Free upgrade

In the ac**tion** for Product:**Pricing**, we're going to go through how you can create a suite of three products – gold, silver and bronze – based on the core product you designed in E02. Once you've done that, you'll be in a position to offer upgrades as a UD.

These are likely to be quite big concessions, so you may only want to provide the upgraded experience for a limited time – say three months – before it downgrades again. This is part of the time-honoured 'drug dealer strategy', where you try to get customers hooked on your wares before whacking the price up. It's not subtle – and most people are alive to it – but it works. Again, honesty and openness are your watchwords here to avoid any erosion of trust.

What might customers get in their upgrade? In the Product:**Pricing** ac**tion**, we'll see what a product suite looks like, but first let's enjoy a Growth Execution Tip.

GROWTH EXECUTION TIP #0414 - SHOULD I ADOPT THE DRUG DEALER STRATEGY?

The discounted first-purchase price - often called the drug dealer strategy - is an accepted way of attracting new customers to a product. In bald terms, the idea is to get them so 'addicted' to using your product that - even when you whack the Product:**Pricing** up - they remain delighted to carry on paying for it, as their experience tells them that the positive benefit hit they get is worth the higher cost.

The problem with this strategy is that a lot of people have been through notional rehab. This is the realisation that they seem to be highly susceptible to these kinds of trials and need to cut back. They vow never to touch any of this stuff again, regardless of how enticing it may seem - the cold turkey just isn't worth it.

Don't let your product fall into this category. Flip it so that it's the 'new gym strategy' with a particular focus on customers being able to exit at any time, with no hidden costs. Invest in genuine support chat boxes with regular webinars and testimonials to show them how to maximise the value so that it's not all self-administered with patchy outcomes.

Push the healthy flexible upside hard; you're using the discount to show customers the good stuff, not sneak in the bad. And the knowledge that they can easily give up is likely to mean that they never feel the need to.

GROWTH EXECUTION TIP #0416 - GIVE TO GET

It's easy to buy business. If you're spending £1.50 to get every £1, you're going to have a lot of takers - and very little time before you go under. So, what's with all of the 'free gifts' that so many businesses throw around?

The critical piece here is the 'give to get'. A classic sales technique, it posits that there is no situation where you should give anything up in a negotiation unless you are able to get something in return for the concession.

Someone wants a discount? Sure, providing they're willing to sign a longer contract. Is a free upgrade available? Sure, in return for a 'share' of the offer, with a recommendation, among their social media followers.

If you're thinking of giving a 'free gift' - a report on the state of your market, perhaps, or a scorecard of a customer's profile in a particular area - then make sure that you're capturing some customer consent to marketing along the way as a bare minimum.

The next thing you have to be doing is putting this data through a very well-understood sales funnel, which tells you how many you are going to need before you sell one of your products. That 'Return on Investment' (ROI) is the key number, the one that tells you whether that 'free gift' is actually the most costly thing you're ever going to have.

ac**tion:** create a product suite

Most people don't want to be cheap. Most people don't want to be flash. The middle-of-the-road is where the majority of a business's clientele aim for – it's why people choose the second bottle of wine on a list at a restaurant rather than the cheapest and distrust the outliers who are too loud or too quiet.

This framing of a middle way plays into your business opportunity, too. If you can create a gold, silver and bronze suite – a luxury, standard and light version of your product – then you're helping people to see the tremendous value that is created from your standard (or 'core' one).

Where do you start in creating a product suite?

First up, make a list of ten features of your product in descending order of value. It may be that you have to stretch a bit here to find enough, so if you need to add in a monthly newsletter or a weekly webinar near the top, then do so – you don't have to deliver it personally, but by going through this exercise, you are challenging your own assumptions around what your value proposition is.

The bottom two features on the list – the least valuable – are going to be your bronze package. These plus the middle five are going to be your silver, and the top three, the most valuable, are going to be added in for your gold.

Let's have a quick look at each in turn, starting with the most important – silver.

Silver package. This is your 'profit engine' which will bear the most similarity to the core product that you defined in Product:**Design** (E02) and is priced according to your thirty-six-month calculations from this element, Product:**Pricing** (E04). As a result, it will be the one that you focus rigorously on getting most customers on to.

In truth, the other two packages are really there to frame this silver product. This 'Goldilocks' option (not too hot and not too cold) is a really strong way to provide the people you are here to serve with the appearance of choice – while framing that choice in such a way that they are highly likely to choose the one that is best for you and your business.

Bronze package. This is the 'entry-level' product, with just two of the seven features that are present in silver. Broadly speaking, this ought to cost 20% of whatever silver is; it should not be free. Giving away any of your actual products for free tells everyone that they're essentially worthless, really. Never, ever do it.

Gold package. Aim to justify a price tag for your premium gold package that is five times whatever silver is. Go nuts. Include concierge services or exclusive hand-made versions. Rarely will you have to deliver on it, so don't waste too much time working out how to build it until you get your first order – there are always some who can't stand less than the best.

Now you have three products from your one – and a strong pricing strategy that lets everyone participate at the level they feel comfortable with. You'll also see your core product take-up grow considerably, as people feel that they're making a choice rather than being offered just one route in.

You can have fun creating names for the products, but ensure that they are in keeping with your Product:**Concept** (E01). And always leave a 'platinum' package in reserve for later – once everyone's upgraded to gold, you'll need it.

resolu**tion**

This element remains one of the most fun to do. If you're not excited by the prospect of creating a thirty-six-month Product:**Pricing** plan, at least the prospect of UDs and a brand-new product suite ought to make it much more entertaining.

We're nearly at the end of your product creation process. There's just one thing left to consider in this discipline – that's what makes you different, your Product:**USP**.

What's unique about you? How can you launch ahead of the competition?

ELEMENT 05

Product:**USP**

defini**tion**

It is a truth universally acknowledged that every business needs something unique about it, otherwise it is on a rather steep and fast track down to oblivion. When your future customers look around to see what's available to help them solve their problem – the one you identified in Product:**Concept** (E01), all those elements ago – their eyes will always be drawn to something fresh and exciting, something different.

Similarly, to keep competitors at bay, your Product:**USP** has to work hard and preserve the gap between you and them. This means that it has to be something flexible as well as different and continue to evolve as those envious of your success come haring after you.

But how do you identify it for your business as it launches? And what's required to protect it from being lifted wholesale by competitors?

The first thing to understand is the make up of a Product:**USP**. Let's start by reminding ourselves what it stands for.

Unique. It's singular – there can be no others sharing this particular attribute with you. This is the main sticking point when you're discovering your USP – how can its permanence be baked into a business at launch and maintained thereafter? The good news is that there is a way – but it needs a clear process of ruling out other options first.

Selling. Your USP can't be something that is simply a feature of your business, like its name. It has to be something that pushes people further down the funnel (see Sales:**Process**, [E11]) towards a successful sale.

Point. Your USP is not a smorgasbord of things that, combined, make a definitively different entity. It's something crystal clear; something that can be articulated or pointed at, reported on or shared in an image on social media.

To surface your Product:**USP**, you're going to have to look back over what you've completed so far. This is the final element of the Product discipline, so after this your product will be as complete as it is going to be pre-launch. Therefore, its Product:**USP** has to be in something that has come through the previous four elements.

Let's take each element in turn and review what it can add to your narrative as a distinct and new entrant into the competitive world you're looking to occupy.

Does your Product:USP = Product:Pricing?

Those who receive my daily Growth Execution Tips via email (you can register at www.growtion.co/tips if you're not getting them yet) have an inkling of my thoughts on Product:**Pricing** as a USP.

Never, ever, let price anywhere near your Product:**USP**.

Let's start with what it makes you look like – it makes you look cheap. Really cheap. And people aren't stupid – they know that if something's cheap, then the chances are that it will be of poor quality. Even if it's not poor quality at this point, it's likely to be pretty soon because the company concerned is not going to be able to afford good stuff in the future if it continues to charge prices like these. What's the point in getting involved with it, except on an ultra short-term basis?

If low pricing is your USP, that's what you'll end up with – short-term customers who aren't with you for the greatness of what you do. They're just here for the cheap deal. And they'll be off like a shot the second someone else goes cheaper than you.

It's also worth a quick peek at what this means from a market perspective, too. You're fresh into this, launching into a space where there is competition for the wallet of your customers. Regardless of whether there is direct competition in terms of what you provide, the opportunity cost of the customer choosing you is that someone else is going to miss out.

That someone is likely to respond, and not usually in a super-welcoming way.

If you come in with a low price as your Product:**USP**, those who are making profit from your customers will slash their prices to match or beat yours in an attempt to smoke you out of the market. They'll have more resources, more patience and be more vested in completely shattering your business. You are picking a fight when you go for price as your Product:**USP** – and, I would gently suggest, it's a fight against multiple well-resourced and entrenched foes who will not let you win.

To recap: never, ever, let price anywhere near your Product:**USP**.

Does your Product:USP = Product:Service?

We're going further back into your Product elements here to discern where you can find your Product:**USP**. In Product:**Service** (E03), we find the people that you are here to serve.

I'm sure you'll recall that the critical thing here is their combination of interests and attributes – the avatars of customer groups, the narratives of which reflect those with the problems you solve. The question regarding Product:**USP** is whether these are people that you alone – uniquely – can provide this solution to.

While it's arguable that there is more rarity in this element than in Product:**Pricing**, it's still a huge stretch to assume that only you are the saviour of your cohort's collective day. There will be multiple 'good enough' facsimiles of what you do to ensure that competition for their custom is fierce – and if these copies are not there yet, they will come charging over the hill as soon as you're successful.

Product:**Service**, then, should not be your Product:**USP**

Does your Product:USP = Product:Design?

Back we go once more to Product:**Design** (E02). Here we do find evidence of uniqueness: the way that you have designed your business from the ground up; the processes that you deploy; the qualitative checks and balances that you'll enrich each future transaction with. These are all likely to be new and different to others out there – for now, at least.

And therein lies the problem with Product:**Design**. Even if it's not possible to exactly replicate how you do what you do, it's certainly possible to copy the 'selling point' bit to the extent that its actual definitive uniqueness is moot.

Does your Product:USP = Product:Concept?

We're left with only one Product element, aren't we? But can Product:**Concept** (E01) really be our Product:**USP**?

Let's see. Is it unique? There's only one of you, so the *why* that you're bringing to this party can only be different to anyone else's because your history is different to anyone else's.

Is it a 'point' and does it 'sell'? Your *why* is a definitive statement, which you can articulate and use to draw in those that you seek to serve. It, therefore, hits both marks.

Yes, your Product:**Concept** is the only realistic Product:**USP** that is going to stay with you, stay unique, stay selling and remain a point of difference between you and your competitors. But how do you maximise it?

Before we find out, let's delve into a couple of relevant Growth Execution Tips.

GROWTH EXECUTION TIP #0510 - EXCEPTIONAL SERVICE IS NOT ENOUGH

You think that your service is second to none, do you? You might be right - for now.

One of the most irritating things about a USP is that the better it is, and the more successful you become as a result, the more everyone else tries to copy it. Therefore, it may become just a 'selling point' pretty quickly.

There's only one way to ensure that your USP remains unique - that's to predicate your business on your **Product:Concept**. This is every business's answer to the question 'Why are you solving this problem?' The combination of the 'problem' and (particularly) 'you' is impossible to replicate. That means that it's your USP for as long as you continue in this business.

Once you start to embed this into your product, your marketing, your sales, you're taking the game away from any scavenging competitors. The people that you're attracting to your solution - be they customers, team members, partners or investors - are there not just because of the service that you provide, but *why* you provide it.

That's the secret to your USP. Now - why are you solving that problem again?

GROWTH EXECUTION TIP #0514 - WHAT IF SOMEONE COPIES MY IDEA?

There is a strong belief - particularly from those involved in its purist pursuit - that Product:**Design** is the one thing that can't be copied.

This is a dangerous conceit.

Design can be copied closely enough, even if your venture feels astonishingly unique. If your business is successful, others will seek to copy it to within as close a line as they possibly can. This may include a calculation, particularly if your competitor owns a larger company whose market is being challenged by your work, regarding how much money (and appetite) you have to sue them. If your competitors decide you're 'little', then you could be faced with a de facto mirror image of your product or service.

What to do? Make sure that your Product:**USP** is more than just the design of your product or service. You need to have a brand over the top of it that stands for something, which draws people in. It's that Product:**Concept** which - whatever you're creating - provides the moat around your business that you need to protect it.

Return, always, to the question 'Why am I solving this problem?' Its answer will be uniquely yours - and it is that uniqueness which no one else can mirror.

action: use Product:**USP** to add culture to your startup

This is a step that many overlook because it's something that generally, as a Founder, you can railroad through if you want. However, if you're smart – and the fact that you're reading or listening to this book suggests that you are – you'll recognise this as your first opportunity to develop 'culture' within your nascent enterprise.

Culture is something that is so hard to create and nurture in any business, let alone a startup, that you need to be looking for it and reinforcing it at every opportunity – starting now.

If your Product:**Concept** (E01) is to become your headline-maker, the thing that makes you different, the idea that drives everything you do, you're going to need to articulate it. This is where that oft-mocked staple of some businesses springs from, the mission statement.

Shy not away from creating one for your business. The reason that it hasn't died out is because it – generally, if done right – works.

Once you've got one, your mission statement needs to be a call-to-arms; a retelling, in sentence form, of the answer to 'Why are we solving this problem?' Then it needs to be shared.

The first people you need to get on board with it are current and future stakeholders in the business. This category includes those who may be indirect stakeholders, such as spouses or significant others. Discovering the additional connection and support that you can generate in these networks by such a simple articulation of intention is a truly wonderful experience. You are likely to be astonished by the extra commitment this clarity brings to you and your business.

Next, involve your senior team and staff. Often, to generate additional camaraderie around your USP, it's fun to invite them to either restate the mission or, with guidance, come to the conclusion of what you and they are here to do on their own. However you gain their buy-in to the project's clarity – and it's possible that it might not be for everyone and some will leave – you're getting a serious cultural underpinning of the endeavour from those who will need to be doing much of the work.

Finally, your customers need to know. We've got a whole discipline committed to this critical phase of your launch and growth – we'll get on to it just as soon as we've brought Product to a close.

resolu**tion**

Going right back to the beginning of the discipline, to the genesis of your product to find its Product:**USP** makes sense. It's who you are that inhabits the DNA of your business.

It's often said that every business eventually comes to look like its CEO, and that's true. You can also apply this to leaders of countries, educational establishments, military units, cults and families. Rather than keeping your Product:**Concept** as an occasionally-revealed, whimsical origins story, make it front and centre of all that you do.

As we now move out of Product into the Marketing discipline, you'll see how increasingly critical your Product:**Concept** decision becomes when you define a brand, narrative, data play, social media game and advertising strategy for your launch. If you don't have a Product:**USP**, you're going to struggle.

If that Product:**USP** is anything other than Product:**Concept**, you're not marketing your own business, you're marketing someone else's.

01
Pc
Product
Concept
02
Pd
Product
Design
03
Ps
Product
Service
04
Pp
Product
Pricing
05
Pu
Product
USP

completion

There you have it – that was the Product discipline of the Growth Execution Formula. By now, you should be fully versed in:

E01 – Product:**Concept.** This is the answer to the question 'Why am I solving this problem?' It has two sides to it – the personal ('I') and the practical ('problem') – and is the most important element in the whole formula as its impact resonates through each and every one of the other elements.

E02 – Product:**Design.** This is the journey that your customer makes from vague interest to delighted advocate. It's created by you and requires feedback from the market at every stage. Beginning with an MVP, you iterate on the reactions you get to its creation and pay great attention to what works, as well as what does not.

E03 – Product:**Service.** This is all about the people that you are here to serve. They've got problems and you've got their solution. To discover who they are, you'll create avatars bringing their demography, interests and beliefs to the fore. Understanding these, you'll be able to ensure that the product you're creating is fit for their purpose.

E04 – Product:**Pricing.** This is the strategy you need to organise not just the launch price of your product, but also its transition over the next three years to your required profitability. You'll plot when to increase prices over time and when to deploy UDs to maximise take-up.

E05 – Product:**USP.** This is the identification of the facet of your venture that is uniquely you. Reflecting the Product:**Concept** that you articulated at the beginning of the Product discipline, you'll create a mission statement for everyone to get behind – stakeholders, team and customers.

Building your product is never going to be easy. If it was, you could be absolutely certain that it would have been done already. It's your unique combination of factors – your ambition, experience, vision, relentlessness, curiosity and flat-out hard work – that's going to make this the success you dream of.

Keep on iterating. Even when you achieve PMF and discover what it's like to see your creation fly off the shelves, always be on the lookout for improvements that need to be made, historical features that need to be jettisoned.

Now it's here, we're going to need to tell people about your product. Ready for some Marketing action?

Let's get growing.

DISCIPLINE TWO
MARKETING

introduction

There are three critical things to remember as you work through the five elements of the Marketing discipline:

1. **Marketing is the heart of your business.** Intra-business anthropomorphism can help to illuminate otherwise hard-to-grasp concepts in your own business. To that end, consider the three disciplines of business growth thus:

    Product: the head. Thoughtful, considered, iterative and concerned with all other body-parts, Product responds to external as much as internal stimuli and is always learning how to make more of an impact for itself and those around it.

    Marketing: the heart. It's all about emotions in this discipline. The job at hand is to appeal to potential customers' core beliefs and drivers; to engage with them on an almost instinctive level and help them to see the solution you've created for them as something that transcends pure logic.

    Sales: the hands. When all of the thinking has been done and the emotion has generated desire, it's time to get practical. How do you actually get this idea done? That's where the artisanal Sales comes into its underrated own – it's put to work in service of the body-whole.

These distinctions are particularly useful as we enter the ethereal Marketing realm, which is far less practical and more emotional than the others. You need to be thinking of this kind of connection to your audience all the way through these five Marketing elements.

2. **You will launch during this discipline.** Surprised? Don't be. Once you get past Marketing:**Content** (E08), there's nothing to stop you. Thanks to your Marketing:**Intel** (E07), you'll know where the people you're going after hang out, you'll know how to communicate with them, and you'll have a Marketing:**Brand** (E06) to summarise why you're here. Then the product itself can go out as an MVP, needing the competitive world to review it and give you feedback.

I often find that entrepreneurs – through no fault of their own, it's a perfectionist thing – can procrastinate over the actual launch itself. If it helps, slap the word 'beta' alongside 'launch' – it does wonders for the confidence in getting your product out there.

3. **Inbound leads are everything.** Marketing has one job: to drive leads for your product into your sales. That's why it sits at the heart of your business and has to be rigorous and ruthless in its pursuit of fresh prospects.

Cold-calling and hopeful-hitting are not going to drive a systemised, scalable business. You need to discover the secret of 'magicking' inbound leads into your sales function. Once you find that, you're in amazing shape simply to rinse them through and repeat.

The Marketing discipline contains five specific elements dedicated to mastering the art of attraction – drawing the people you are here to serve ever closer towards you, so that you can entice them to commit through sales. It's an area that will reward creativity and lateral thinking, as people are incredibly wary of having their attention diverted into something new. They need to trust you, first and foremost. And that begins with consistent, coherent messaging from a Marketing:**Brand** they share principles with.

Your brand is shorthand for all the good that you do. How can you build one cost-effectively?

ELEMENT 06

Marketing:**Brand**

defini**tion**

The easiest way to think about Marketing:**Brand** is that it's your shorthand for Product:**Concept** (E01).

Every attribute that you have imbued your product with – its reason for existence, the coolness of its design, the people it's here to serve, its pricing-levels – needs to be visible in its Marketing:**Brand**. And if you think that's a significant amount of heavy lifting for one element to handle, you're right.

This is a huge responsibility, one that it is difficult to overstate. As a result, Marketing:**Brand** is one element that I would – if you have any budget at all – encourage you to invest in. There are other options, which we will get to in this section, but unless you, or a co-founder, are an ex-creative director for a brand, there is no substitute for a professional designer for your Marketing:**Brand**.

You can find recommendations regarding available resources for this task at the grow**tion** website at www.growtion.co. The general amount you can look to spend is between £5,000 and £20,000, depending on the level you want to go in at.

The minimum outcome is a document called *Brand Guidelines*. These are your go-to answers to every single question you will ever have for the life of your business, covering as a minimum:

- Iconography (including logo)
- Fonts
- Colours
- Additional images
- Strapline/catchphrase

Again, I can't emphasise enough how much time, effort, thought and fixes you'll save by having such a document produced professionally. Our *Brand Guidelines* were put together by 10creative.co.uk and – many years later – we still use them regularly to keep everything tight. And nothing has changed – the 'pudding-eating' proves a great, complete **Marketing:Brand** design.

That's the gold standard. If you can afford it, commit to prioritising this and – with just one quick detour through the 'ac**tion**' section of this element, where you can sense-check your chosen name – skip to E07.

For everyone else – fear not. This section is going to walk you through all of the requirements to build your own **Marketing:Brand** from scratch.

It's a significant undertaking, but the rewards for not scrimping on any area of it are huge.

Iconography

Your logo is the visual finger-click that makes people snap towards you and form a swift judgement on what they see. The list of great logos is long and will not trouble us here. What they all share, though, will – and it's probably not the thing that you may think it is.

Each and every one of the best logos is for a business that has an instantly recognisable *why*: its Product:**Concept** (E01). It's not that it's irrelevant what the business's logo is – although it almost is; it's that its ethos, role, willingness to serve is such that one sight of its logo inspires full confidence that it's the company that will solve your problem (or not, if it is targeted at others).

Getting too hung-up on a logo for your product is not time well-spent. You have plenty of other things to do, so head to a logo-maker website (examples at www.growtion.co) and experiment with what you find. More often than not, these logos will be abstract and unrelated to your specific name or field, but there is no significant downside to this – people recognise the brand attributes that you ascribe to an icon more than the icon itself, as Nike's swoosh and Ferrari's prancing horse will attest.

Fonts

The biggest regret business owners I work with have about fonts is not settling on ones that can be replicated easily on the web as well as in print. There are fewer in the former camp, so it's worth starting with a search for these.

Don't spend over-long on this at launch – you just need a typeface that's clear and readable. Raleway and Montserrat are a couple of good ones. Designers will tell you that you need a complementary one that is different for headers, but I think that's over-engineering it. Wait until you've launched successfully before considering such nice-to-haves.

Colours

Obsess about these. There is nothing quite as striking as a consistent, coherent colour palette. Some super-smart sites have really good auto-generated combinations (examples at www.growtion.co) and you can instantly see how they'll work with your name and iconography.

Go for one with a stand-out contrasting colour for the main theme, as this will become the one you'll use for website buttons and hyperlink addresses.

Additional images

You'll need some stock images that visually guide potential customers in what they are being asked to do or consider at each point of their journey with your product. A header image – something related to the product you sell – is important for websites and as backgrounds for title pages of documents and presentations. Taking some arty photos with your smartphone around the office, or close-ups of items on your home desk or outside in bright light, helps to build a library of visually connected images you can deploy in different settings as you build out your presence.

A single hi-res headshot of you provides the answer to a lot of questions you'll get about social media accounts and 'About Us' pages. It should at least be torso and up, against a plain background and not too formal or fierce.

Strapline/catchphrase

This is a bit of a controversial one, so bear with me.

The way that people think about your business post launch will be influenced by all of the above, and also what they read, hear and watch in Marketing:**Content** (E08). If all that is summarised into one pithy strapline or catchphrase, it can really help them to understand what you're about.

At grow**tion**, the catchphrase is 'Let's get growing'. While it isn't baked into the iconography as a true strapline would be, it appears with insistent regularity in our daily *Growth Execution Tips*, weekly *Growth Execution Newsletter* and *Growth Execution Podcast*, the training courses in the *Growth Execution Academy*... you get the picture. By over-familiarising people with it, we ensure it sticks like an earworm jingle, and thus does its job all the better.

The idea with any strapline or catchphrase is to frame the **Product:Concept**, to distil its essence into a small combination of words. It may be that these don't come together instantly, or quickly, or possibly ever, but do keep thinking about your strapline or catchphrase when you're out on a run or in the shower. If you do, it's likely to come eventually.

The value of repetition is hard to measure, but it is clear in the examples of those that have got it extraordinarily right. 'Just do it', 'Every little helps', 'Finger-lickin' good', 'Love it or hate it', 'Because you're worth it'... all of these straplines are instantly recognisable. What's yours?

Your **Marketing:Brand** will evolve, but you need to make the big decisions now and stick with them. Colours, name, icon – in five years' time, the closer your brand is to the attributes that you launch with right now, the more successful you will be.

I guarantee it.

GROWTH EXECUTION TIP #0605 - BRAND IS SHORTHAND FOR WHO YOU ARE

To get your product or service out into the world in the most efficient way possible, you need to pause for a second. Think about the brands that stand out to you, the ones that make a promise from just their icon or their typeface, their hashtag or their colour scheme. These are speaking to you quickly, effectively, consistently and coherently. They're doing it effortlessly, because they know who they are. And that comes out shorthand through their brand.

Use this time to ensure that your brand reflects who you are. Consistency is critical; it's the organisations that only give a cursory nod to coherence that are forgettable. (I'm sure you will be able to think of examples yourself, although they may not come easily to mind, for obvious reasons.) A lack of consistency will not build a business fast.

Get your colour combination together; look for inspiration from numerous brand colour scheme sites, accessible from a simple Google search. I'd always go for five shades, at least one light and one dark, plus one that contrasts with the core colour, such as the pink in grow**tion** www.growtion.co.

Choose a typeface and stick with it, forever. Montserrat is good and free, as are Work Sans and Raleway.

Use your icon and the way that you write your brand name consistently, but creatively. All of these elements - including the tone of voice that you use in all that you say - build trust in you and what you are here to do. Your business needs this.

GROWTH EXECUTION TIP #0612 - DO I REALLY HAVE TO BOTHER WITH CONSISTENT FONTS?

In all of the challenges of making a business grow, there are some things that you can do which have an outsized positive impact. One of those is ensuring consistency.

Humans are programmed to notice tiny differences in case they progress into a significant 'threat'. If you don't give consistency any conscious thought at all, your potential audience's recognition that something is not 'as expected' will cause them to pause. The resultant impact on momentum is devastating to SME growth.

Do yourself and your business a big favour and don't shortcut on typeface consistency. If anything stands as a surrogate for your ability to manage the full range of requirements of running a business, your attention to this detail could be it. Remember this: disorganised typeface = disorganised business.

Attend to it - and make sure that everyone else knows how important consistency is here. You're likely to be amazed at how other things become instantly aligned.

ac**tion**: choose your Marketing:**Brand** name

One of the things that entrepreneurs love to get to quickly is the name of their product. It starts out as a project that requires a word or two to summarise it, and that generally becomes the brand name, regardless of how much thought went into it (which is sometimes, though by no means always, quite a lot).

Whatever your 'working title' is for your product, there are a few questions to cover off before you settle upon and fix its name.

How unique is it? What happens when you type it into a search engine? Who owns the .com of the core word/words? Is the localised suffix (eg .co.uk) available?

What does it sound like? If it was spoken on a podcast or a radio advert, would anyone have the faintest idea what URL they'd need to type in to find you?

Are the social media handles available? The idea is to have the same combination of characters for each platform if possible.

What does it look like when hashtagged? Remember when Susan Boyle's media team decided, while publicising the release of her new collection of songs, that #susanalbumparty would be a perfect combination of words to hashtag in all lower-case letters together? Be careful out there.

What else is being used? Anything close? It's worth registering the Trademark – it costs a few hundred pounds, but it will flag up any potential conflicts and alert those who might complain to do so early.

There is nothing quite like spending months pre-launch with a particular project name, collecting all the visuals together and getting to the verge of launch... then having to start again. Believe me, I was there. Just before a New Year launch in 2016, I received a letter on Christmas Eve 2015 saying that there was an objection to the brand name – but I didn't see it, let alone open it until 2 January, by which time my team had run really hard to get everything together. But I'd still rather that than have to remove the name from everything post launch.

You are going to have to live with your brand name for a long time, if everything goes according to plan at and after launch. Everything you can do now to minimise regret will stop you coming to loathe it in due course.

You need to love your brand name and care for it. Start now.

resolu**tion**

Your Marketing:**Brand** will become the most-recognisable element of your entire business post launch. This carries with it a huge weight of responsibility – it has to be right.

It's not like a Product:**Design** (E02) or Product:**Pricing** (E04) that can vary without huge (and costly) collateral damage, operationally and reputationally. Your brand is out there, accruing value as you demonstrate your business's strengths. If it disappears suddenly or changes unrecognisably, you've got issues that are far more damaging than colour palette changes on your website.

You can get a professional designer to help with your Marketing:**Brand** and save yourself a lot of time and effort further down the line. This is a strong recommendation – if you have any budget for marketing, dropping £5k+ on this is well worthwhile.

If not – and it's entirely reasonable to choose to go it alone – then prioritise getting the brand name right, use some great online resources to provide the icon, typefaces and colours for free, and see if you can summarise your Product:**Concept** in a catchphrase or strapline.

Once you've got all this together, you're ready to start digging deep to find the people you're here to serve – those who need to see your consistent, coherent brand the most. And that's what we're going to explore next in Marketing:**Intel** (E07).

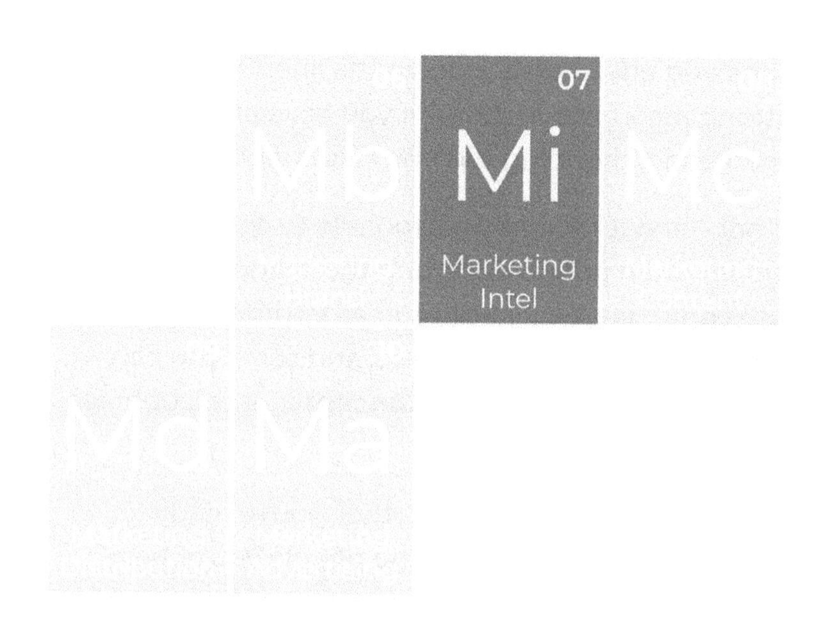

How can you target the right people effectively at launch?

ELEMENT 07

Marketing:**Intel**

defini**tion**

It's been a while – in Product:**Service** (E03), four elements ago, to be precise – since we've really paid attention to who you're here for. That focus elsewhere has been important to take you and your launch forward, but if you're to succeed with the people that you are here to serve, it needs to end here. We need to refocus on them.

Welcome to Marketing:**Intel**.

If you throw too much marketing out at loads of people without thinking about whether they're really going to be that interested, you will be wasting a huge amount of time, energy and money. This element is all about your future customers:

Who are they?

What are they like?

What are they thinking?

How do you find them?

Let's start at the beginning with:

Who are they?

Back in Product:**Service** (E03), we looked at the potential audience for your product so that you could craft it with them in mind. In particular, we looked at:

- **Market quality:** luxury, volume or mid-top market?
- **Gender:** male, female or neither?
- **Age/life stage:** teenager, boomer, somewhere in between?
- **Interests:** music, sport, art, TV, gaming or others?
- **Geography:** hyper-local, global or something in between?
- **Beliefs:** religious, political, philosophical and/or moral?

What are they like?

In general, the answer to this question can be quite broad. Any collection of humans, regardless of a shared interest, will contain wildly divergent personalities that are difficult to summarise. Difficult, yes; impossible, no.

There are traits that are common to a majority of those interested in certain things. Librarians may like quiet – it is certainly unlikely that they love a lot of noise. Car enthusiasts may like speed; birdwatchers may like picnics. Sportswomen may like competition, compliance officers less so.

Pick three traits and consider which are likely to be positive or negative to your target audience. Then you can start to get into their heads.

What are they thinking?

This is the key to unlocking the audience that you're targeting. If you can really and truly decipher their motivation, then you are going to be a long way down the line towards achieving your goal of serving them well.

The things to look out for are, more often than not, the things that clearly get them emotional. For example, if you tell an opera-goer that you love a particular aria, you are signalling that you're part of the same club and their emotional response to you will change their willingness to buy.

It is this emotionality – unstructured, unfiltered and mostly illogical – that will be the ultimate lever that you can pull to get people to buy.

How do you find them?

This is a critical piece of work as it provides the answers to the questions 'Where do they hang out?' in Marketing:**Distribution** (E09) and 'Where should you advertise?' in Marketing:**Advertising** (E10).

Let's take a deeper detour into the world of interaction opportunities for your fresh startup. It's not just social media; there are also membership clubs, sporting events and political conferences that your potential audience might attend. What you're looking for here is not a definitive plan of how to contact them – not just yet – but a wide view of where you need to make sure you are present to minimise Marketing:**Advertising** costs and maximise Marketing:**Distribution** outreach.

Now let's examine the profiles of various social media platforms for their relevance to what you want to do, before taking a look at which offline activity might attach itself to success for you.

Facebook. Pretty much the grandparent of social media these days, Facebook is far more than just somewhere to wish people you've lost touch with a happy birthday. The amount of data that this platform holds on the world in general is pretty fearsome (if you're a privacy campaigner), but also amazing (if you're launching your own business around about now).

What Facebook has is a 'Group' function which allows you to join somewhere that caters for your kind of audience, and then create your own where you can interact with people who are interested in what you have to offer. These groups are easy to set up but can take a while to get going properly. Broadly, you need between 200 and 500 members before your group becomes self-sustaining – and until then, it's almost all up to you to keep it going.

LinkedIn. Interesting from a B2B point of view – for anything else, it's pretty dull. For businesses, one of the best things about LinkedIn is its 'Search' function. From the names of individuals, to people with the same job titles, to those who hang out in the same groups, you can pretty much pick your audience and get involved.

If you register your interests as hashtags in your own profile, then you can be alerted any time someone mentions one in a post. Swinging across to make a pertinent point can significantly increase your visibility among those that you seek to serve, so doing this regularly is a good use of time.

Twitter. It is hard to discover and track a community or target audience on Twitter, unless you are looking for one polarised by its opposition to another. Even then, there is always a risk that you will get dragged unwittingly into something that is only going to distract you from your purpose and/or portray you in a dim light. If something you post is taken in the wrong way, it can harm your potential connection with your audience. At this point, Twitter is best avoided.

Instagram. Useful for a Millennial and younger market, for highly-visual products and/or those who love #hashtaggingeverything, Instagram should be in the mix for use in your Marketing:**Distribution**, particularly as its parent Facebook has united the ability to segment across both platforms.

TikTok. The 'nipper' of the social media family. The fact that my twenty-year-old niece was bemoaning all the 'kids' using it tells you what you need to know about TikTok's demographics. As with every social media platform before it, it's becoming more adult, but it will take a while before it becomes essential as part of the broad mid-market demographic's regular lives.

Offline. Clubs are the offline version of and precursor to online groups. Whether we do it via fan clubs, sports clubs, book clubs or social clubs, our human desire to band together based on common interest is still strong.

Finding the offline collective that can provide you with Marketing:**Intel** is more straightforward these days, when you can (ironically, perhaps) find almost all of them online. Whether the members will welcome someone who has a potential motive to sell to them is unlikely, so most of your hard work is probably better done from behind your keyboard.

Soon, it will be ac**tion** time – just how do you engage with groups full of members who are your target audience? Before we have a look at the answer, let's enjoy some relevant Growth Execution tips.

GROWTH EXECUTION TIP #0701 – THE DATA OUT THERE ABOUT YOU IS SCARY

Marketing:**Intel** is focused around the sort of data that you understand about your particular customers.

It is the case these days that there is much information, much intelligence out there on all of us. You can google pretty much anybody you like – you've probably done it with regards to recruiting and interviewing people. I certainly have (sorry, anybody who has been interviewed by me). You look at everything you can possibly find on their Twitter feed or Facebook profile – it's actually a bit scary how much is out there about you and the people you are going to meet. You can find out what a potential client had for breakfast. And all of that information, all that data is affecting decisions that people make.

In a similar way, people will be googling your business, understanding what it is that you have been doing in your past. Who hasn't looked on LinkedIn and seen all the different jobs that people have been doing and made judgements on them as a result?

We as a species consider ourselves quite smart and intelligent, so we will always go and find things out. And we will make snap judgements on people from things that we see.

GROWTH EXECUTION TIP #0708 - HOW DID ZOOPLA USE A LEAD MAGNET TO DRIVE GROWTH?

'Lead magnets' are services that draw people into giving their data to you because they want to get something that you have.

Zoopla pioneered the 'Automated Valuation Model' for homes. You could (and still can) get an estimate of what any property in the UK is worth from the site. All you have to do is provide a bit of information about yourself in return.

What's your lead magnet? What can you provide from your product or service that is of value to your target market - those that you seek to serve - and will start them on the journey with you? A great resource for this is Typeform[7] - you can create really interesting questionnaires that can give respondents a score on whatever you like. Try grow**tion**'s one (www.growtion.co/scorecard). It's free, fun and shows what's possible.

You need to capture people at the start of their decision-making process and make sure that you're front and centre of their minds. Zoopla grew a business worth billions on the back of its lead magnet - it's worth you having a look at one for your business, too.

---

7 www.typeform.com

action: create a Marketing:**Intel** scorecard

How can you encourage your target audience to share their data with you? By making it fun.

A scorecard is a smart, interactive series of questions that enables a potential client to get something of value to them after giving their responses. Essentially what you're doing is gathering information on the client through them answering questions which are pertinent to you and the product that you wish to sell to them. In return, they get a number – a score – that is automatically calculated based upon their answers. This is something that you input yourself into the multiple-choice answers to each question, building to an overall total reflecting some aspect of the potential client or their business that is relevant to your product. You can see a great example of this at www.growtion.co/scorecard.

The real benefit of a scorecard is that it provides an in-depth summary of the potential client's details, which you can use specifically to target them. You can also use it to aggregate so that you can see a much wider picture of the sector that you're seeking to serve. In turn, this provides you with the ability not only to be targeted in your provision of assistance to each individual customer – a gold product requirement, for example – but also to use the metadata gleaned from these scorecards to continually interrogate your product, systems and processes to ensure that they're maximising opportunities.

A scorecard can really change the game when it comes to Marketing:**Intel** and your understanding of your audience's needs.

resolu**tion**

Now that you know where to find the people you are here to serve and how to approach them, you need to have something to say – that's where the next element, Marketing:**Content**, comes in. You're likely to recall from the start of the Marketing discipline that it's after that pivotal element – the eighth of the fifteen – that you'll be ready to get your MVP out.

It's all about trust – we've seen the benefits of narrowing your audience down to its core niche; now you have to get your potential clients' attention and commitment to what you're doing. Providing some of them with the MVP is going to be a key way of achieving that.

People buy new services and products based on trust – how do you build this quickly?

ELEMENT 08

Marketing:**Content**

defini**tion**

Why do people spend so much time creating and consuming Marketing:**Content**?

It's not a question often asked – we tend to just get on with it. Producing and consuming, consuming and producing. But when you stop to think about your own habits – the news sites you visit, the social media apps that have notifications switched on on your phone, the streaming video services you watch – it's clear that there is a fundamental human driver to connect and, less often, contribute to that connection through stories and information.

What's all this connectivity giving us? Trust.

From the earliest swampy steps our ancestors made, through the sharing of rudimentary tools or recipes, and on to 'Breaking News' exclusives on tablets, successful humans – ie those who survived long enough to pass their genes on down to us – have been content consumers. Every nugget of information we glean from another could be the piece that saves our lives in some unforeseen circumstance in the future, so we gather it, magpie-like, from as many places as we can. But, of course, there's just way too much to internalise it all, so we have developed ways of filtering information that enables us to, essentially, continue living without being overwhelmed by conflicting-data overload. This filter can most easily be expressed as the word 'trust'.

Trust is a continuum, affected by a number of different facets – but almost all of these are related to the conveyor of the information who's asking to be trusted. Who is this person? How do they relate to me and what is their motivation for sharing this with me, right now?

A family member with whom we share a close bond will, naturally, be towards the higher 'trustworthy' end of this spectrum. Those who have lied to us before will sludge towards the 'untrustworthy' end. Complete strangers could be just below the midpoint, although they can raise their trustworthiness by demonstrating membership of a wider group that we are already aligned with (and have high trust in).

What's the relevance of all this for our journey through Marketing:**Content**? This element is essentially the one where you learn how to build trust. Assuming that you have got your Product:**Concept** (E01) honest and true – again, that is an element that you just can't skip – then the job of work here is to ensure that you're trusted by those you seek to serve, so that they buy from you.

Simple, right? If only.

It is so difficult to create, articulate, and then launch a consistent and coherent Marketing:**Content** campaign that *The Launch Handbook* is going to make you do it before you launch your MVP in beta. If you do it any other way – launch the product before you have articulated its value via Marketing:**Content** – then you're wasting the moment. You're essentially consigning your beta launch to a muddled relaunch in a few months when you *have* got your messaging together.

Let's get ready for a powerful beta launch by maximising the efficiency of your Marketing:**Content** output, building a credible foundation upon which to launch your MVP. The first thing to understand is the trio of core media that you can harness for your communication outreach.

Audio

One of the major benefits of audio content is its flexibility – you can listen to it while you're doing a bunch of other things, such as running, commuting on the train/bus, walking the dog, waiting at the dentists' or driving to another meeting. What it lacks in complete attention, it makes up for in flexibility.

A reason that it's so important in your suite of communications is that it complements the other two, both of which tend to be more immersive and require additional concentration to get the most out of them.

Video

This is the gold standard of comms. Until recently, it was generally considered to be the preserve of huge corporations or well-moneyed startups. No longer.

You can video yourself in astonishingly high resolution, upload the film to your tablet and use a cheap everyday app to add music, subtitles and image overlays, and bookends. It's phenomenally cost-effective these days, but that does bring with it a challenge, too – loads of sub-standard videos are now making their way on to the screens of your target audience without the quality control that you're going to put in place. That means your videos need to have as much additional context and strong content as possible.

Text (print/on screen)

It's amazing to think that the technology to mass-print has only been available for a few hundred years – and that mass education, including reading, is even more recent. Even though text is the grandparent of these three comms methods, it still carries resonance – though far less than when it was the only real medium in town. Humans tend towards efficiency (others call it 'laziness') and listening to something or watching something requires less effort than reading it – but text still needs to have your focus, as it can outlast the others.

With the trio of communications methods clear, now you need to populate each with a consistent and coherent message. You're here to build trust, and that means you need to repeat yourself regularly.

One of the best pieces of advice I have ever received is this: always remember, even if you are so overly-familiar with your Marketing:**Content** that you think it needs a complete refresh, that there are many new clients who are coming to it cold, for the first time, every day. Going wildly off-piste and constantly throwing out new and conflicting messages doesn't make you sound edgy; it makes you sounds like you're unconfident in your Marketing:**Content**'s ability to stand up for itself – and that the rest of it's probably not worth paying attention to.

What is the best way to ensure that your Marketing:**Content** is credible, coherent and consistent? It's by repurposing as much as you possibly can.

Podcasts

These are great ways to build credibility. Even if you don't have a reliable audience of listeners, the fact that you are creating this Marketing:**Content** regularly will draw in many at least once. The ability your targets have to hear what you're talking about while they do other things gives audio a unique impact, and podcasts are a great way to get people dipping in and out.

A favourite tactic of mine is to *video* the podcast episodes and release bitesize chunks of them on a regular basis (I do mine each working day as a daily Growth Execution Tip, which you can see in the Growth Execution Group on Facebook). Visuals are highly compelling – our ancestors were used to storytelling at campfire-time, so we're super-primed to believe this medium more than most others. Video is really cost-effective to make these days, too.

Obtaining caption or subtitle files from the videos that you've created then provides transcripts of the original audio that you produced. These can be edited into a series of **blogs** around the same topic –

a good example of this can be found at www.growtion.co/blog.

Trust is the key here, of course, and you can't drop the ball in structure and process in Marketing:**Content**. If you promise a weekly podcast, then you'd better deliver, or it will undo much of your hard work.

By focusing on these three specific methods of communication, you are building an ecosystem of repurposed Marketing:**Content** which will reinforce as well as reassure. However your future audience comes across your messaging, it will be exactly the same and provide clear articulation of your Product:**Concept** in multiple ways.

GROWTH EXECUTION TIP #0801 - CONSISTENCY AND AUTHENTICITY IN MARKETING:CONTENT

Authenticity is easy to spot, isn't it?

It's the brand that effortlessly exhibits the same values, ideas and behaviours that you expect it to. It never veers from that steady path, and this enables you to choose to either love it or hate it. You opt-in or opt-out.

Many businesses want to appeal too widely, and so they can't be authentic for any one particular audience. This means that they fail to capture a dedicated customer base, instead attracting those with little loyalty who are motivated more by convenience or price - and will leave as soon as something more convenient or cheap comes along.

That is not going to help you thrive in this market.

Instead, go back to your Product:**Concept** and answer the question 'Why are you solving this problem?' Dig deep. Once you know, your Marketing:**Content** - what you put out into the world through writing, audio and video - becomes astonishingly straightforward.

Because it's authentic. Because it's you.

GROWTH EXECUTION TIP #0817 - TEXT, AUDIO OR VIDEO?

Working out what to say is one thing - working out how to say it is another.

The medium that you choose to distribute your message is critical to how it is received. Text tends to favour a considered, perhaps older, audience. What you say in it is likely to be longer form, requiring more thought and allowing the recipient to go back over it carefully and identify the key points that resonate.

Audio is great for something that is more ambient and repetitive. Something that has a broad theme which drops from consciousness to subconsciousness with the repetition of key words or phrases, like a favourite radio station jingle or song chorus.

Video requires more concentration and effort, so needs to be shorter and pithier - up to ninety seconds for impactful, sharp messages that generate action, but also allow you the complete range of additional techniques. Clearly, audio is there, but you can also add text subtitles or captions, so that you can still communicate to people in environments where noise is not appropriate. Generally speaking, the newer the medium, the shorter the messaging should be.

Always remember that you need eleven touches in all before someone trusts you enough to buy. Keep experimenting with the medium but keep the message consistent.

ac**tion**: construct your Marketing:**Content** acronym IP

Ideas can be hard to grasp. Yes, you've worked tirelessly to ensure that you've got a structured message and core Product:**Concept** that really resonate. But sometimes even the perception of complexity is enough to put your desired audience off from drinking deep from your Marketing:**Content** well. If your product finds itself in the position that it's so good/revolutionary/complete/complex that it requires a long explanation before people understand it, you need to think about an acronym intellectual property (IP).

This is where you choose an acronym that stands for a simplified description of your product – for example, specific, measurable, achievable, relevant, time-bound (SMART) goals or a homemade example, the Home-schooled Unified Sports Teams of Lafayette (HUSTL) method, and then make it your IP.

Where do you start? Have a review of your work in Product:**Pricing** (E04), as that's where you listed out the ten features that make up your putative gold/silver/bronze product suite. Can you make any combination of these features into an acronym? Alternatively, go back to Product:**Design** (E02) and work on defining some of the actual process steps into single words that can then be 'acronymised'.

The reason for doing this is to provide simplicity for the potential client in the complex world that they live in. So much comes at them on a daily basis, if you can parse a linear and direct understanding of what you offer, you remove friction from their decision-making and speed up success for you and your launch.

Once you have an acronym, build out the IP behind it. Each of the letters, or stages, of your acronym needs to have a (roughly equally weighted, if possible) basket of value ascribed to it. This is the IP that sits within your business – the protected formula or secret sauce which makes your solution to the client's problem unique – and uniquely desirable as a result.

There's another benefit to having a unique and distinctive acronym IP – the value of your business, should you come to sell it or look to gain investment in it, is considerably enhanced by something visibly and obviously unique to you.

Have a play around with acronyms and how they might dovetail with your Product:**Concept** (E01). Structure around your Marketing:**Content** can be much more readily laid out and grasped if there is a clear journey that the customer needs to go on.

resolu**tion**

This is one of the fatter elements, in that it requires a visibly large volume of work to be done within it, but much of what's needed is really an understanding of the skill of repurposing. You don't have to keep repeating the same thing all the time; you just need to keep repurposing the same thing all the time.

Adding in an acronym IP can really make things easy for you and your future customers, particularly as you're then able to structure different messaging so that it remains fresh even if it is about the same product.

Now that you have enough Marketing:**Content** – and you have honed it so that it's easily repeatable and repurposable – you can start longer conversations with those you wish to help you with the MVP. Up to this point, you would have been launching it without the key messages around it that will ensure you get genuine feedback on the product as is, rather than interminable questions about why and how it's needed.

Assuming that you're now overflowing with ideas about Marketing:**Content** – if not dripping in the actual content itself – we need to talk about what you're going to do with it. How do you ensure that it's reaching the audience you identified in Marketing:**Intel** (E07)?

That's what Marketing:**Distribution** (E09) is for.

How do you make use of the most cost-effective marketing channels, social media and public relations (PR)?

ELEMENT 09

Marketing:**Distribution**

defini**tion**

If there is one thing that's even more frustrating than not having enough Marketing:**Content** (E08), it's having loads of Marketing:**Content** but no idea where it's all supposed to go.

That's what this element, Marketing:**Distribution**, is here to help you plan for. Importantly, it is different from Marketing:**Advertising** (E10), the next element, in one key feature – it does not carry with it a variable cost. Marketing:**Advertising**, as we shall see, is a scalable return on investment (ROI) which is going to make it straightforward – once you know what works – to grow your startup quickly when excess funds become available.

Marketing:**Distribution** is the equivalent of asymmetrical warfare – it doesn't matter how much money you have – guerrilla tactics and extravagant use of free tools and platforms provide you with inexpensive access to the market you seek to serve. At its heart, it's the socialist to Marketing:**Advertising**'s capitalist.

This does not mean that Marketing:**Distribution** is completely free. Anything that requires time and effort cannot be so, but once you have it structured and planned, there is little additional cost. That's why this element has an outsized impact on the success of your launch. Without a shadow of a doubt, the more work you do in this element, preparing the ground and repeatedly expressing your Product:**Concept** (E01), the more success you will have overall.

To build trust, you've created a reservoir of highly relevant and consistent Marketing:**Content** (E08) to draw in your target clients. But how often do you have to speak to them, repeat yourself, before they really do trust you enough to buy from you? It's the next obvious question – and luckily, there is an outfit that has run the numbers. It happens to one of the biggest companies in the world: Google.

Google says that you have to focus hard on just three numbers: eleven, seven, four.[8]

On average, Google says, people need to be 'touched' by your Marketing:**Brand** (E06) **eleven times** before they will buy from you. That means you have to show up in a combination of different environments eleven times before they'll see you as

[8] Jacqui Pretty, 'How to pre-sell your prospects with a book', Dent Blog (27 April 2015), www.keypersonofinfluence.com/pre-sell-prospects-book, accessed 14 March 2021

credible from a quantitative point of view. Does that mean that you can just ping the same advert into their eyeballs eleven times in an hour and then the cash is going to start rolling in? If only. That's why the next number, seven, is here.

Seven hours. Mmm. Sounds like a lot, right? This is the total number of hours that the average consumer – and you'll have identified the ideal ones in Marketing:**Intel** (E07) – needs to spend with a Marketing:**Brand** before they will buy. These hours can be spent consuming webinars, videos, meetings, articles, podcasts, exhibitions – you name it, but it needs to have longevity. Essentially, this is the bit where your potential customers stare at you long and hard to see if you blink and go against what you've said before.

Again, the strength of your Product:**Concept** gives you the confidence and insurance that you're not going to fall down on this. Every minute of the 420 that make up your seven hours will be consistently and coherently on message, because it's true. And therefore trustworthy.

There is a final clarifier around the seven hours and eleven touches: they can't all be in the same medium. Banging out eleven videos of forty minutes in length will get you past your seven hours but won't convince your audience – people are too smart for that these days. They need to see your trustworthiness and consistency translated across different media to check that what you write in a blog is what they see in a video and hear in an interview.

This is the kicker – the one that is most easily overlooked because it's more complex that the quantitative and qualitative previous two. But to maximise your ability to reach your audience – and get them to trust you – you are going to have to get some media variety in your life.

If you've already created audio (podcast), video and text (blog) in Marketing:**Content**, these provide three of the **four** environments that you need. But what of the fourth? How can you further enhance your messaging in another different environment?

The one that I recommend here as the fourth environment is the same thing that should be the call to action (CTA) in every other piece of Marketing:**Distribution** you send out – it's your website. Your website needs to be the spine of your business that pulls in your product, marketing and sales. By using it to harness all of the Marketing:**Content** pieces that you create, you are once more repurposing the core efforts that you've made into something that becomes bigger than the sum of its parts.

Needless to say, the fact that you're reusing the same podcast across each of the four environments ensures that all seven hours and eleven touches of your messaging is consistent and coherent. And that means you're never going to say something that conflicts with what you've said elsewhere. It's all trustworthy.

Now that you have all of your Marketing:**Content** (E08) and you understand the numbers to convert prospects into clients, you can start to build a plan around what you need these points of contact to look like. In the ac**tion** for this element, you'll learn how to build a strategy and a full calendar that achieves this. In the meantime, we're going to look at the more tactical options for Marketing:**Distribution** to get your message out there with little or no cost.

Getting involved

In Marketing:I**ntel** (E07), you identified the most appropriate places to find your future clients, and started watching them and reading a lot of their comments, building an understanding of how they think and what they want. It's that understanding that's now going to help you to connect on a more granular level with them.

In these forums and groups, there are numerous opportunities for you to answer questions regarding your area of expertise. Having spent much of the last element compressing and refining your messaging, you'll have fine-tuned your ability to contribute to debates regarding your specialism confidently and pointedly.

It's time to get involved in these groups. Sticking your head above the parapet in this way can feel quite daunting at first – I know many entrepreneurs who still retain a fear of getting involved in awkward conversations as a result. But don't worry – you can elegantly back away from any that become toxic, and the majority of those looking on will be alive to who takes responsibility for interactions becoming uncomfortable. They'll be more impressed that you're involved than disappointed that you've ended up in a conversation with a troublemaker.

Another **Marketing:Distribution** avenue to consider is PR. A quick word of warning – there are a lot of practitioners of the dark arts of PR who will tell you they need a few months of sky-high fees before their magic can work. At this point in your business's life, give them a swerve. If you can generate some PR for a particular event yourself – a partnership in **Sales:Collaboration** (E12), say, or a milestone hit in **Sales:Goals** (E13) – then do it solo, but don't expend too much energy here just yet. There may be time for it in the future, but not now.

GROWTH EXECUTION TIP #0924 - HOW DO I BUILD TRUST?

From the second you put your business out there, you have made a promise to your future customers. You are now on the hook to deliver.

If you fail to do what you say that you will - the product is late or shonky, there is no consistency in the delivery, and/or it is not as complete as described - then you will lose trust. On the back of that, you will lose customers, revenue and potentially your company over the medium term.

The good news is that the inverse is also true. All it takes to create and build trust is consistency. You have to keep those promises.

Work out what you are comfortable delivering. Remember that it has to reflect your **Product:Concept** ('Why am I solving this problem?'), and it has to be interesting and different enough for people to pay attention. Then diarise what you are going to do, when, and do it. Every. Single. Time. There are so few businesses that do this consistently, you will stand out straight away as a result.

Do the work to understand what your customers need - the problem and its solution. Then deliver on it regularly with the conviction that comes from that understanding.

Make and keep your promises. In business, as in life, trust really is as simple as that.

GROWTH EXECUTION TIP #0914 – WHAT ARE GOOGLE'S FOUR ENVIRONMENTS?

Google loves data. It's essentially what keeps one of the world's most valuable businesses in colourful typefaces. So, when it shares some with us lowly mortals, we ought to pay attention.

In this case, it's the number four.

Four is the 'average number of environments' that your Marketing:**Brand** needs to show up in before customers are ready to buy from you. This basically means four different media – a blog would count as one, for example and a video, face-to-face meeting, podcast another three.

The reason it's four? As ever, it's all about trust.

People don't buy – and they particularly don't buy remotely – if they don't trust what they're going to get, so they cast around for things that confirm – or conflict with – their initial thoughts regarding you. If there is only one channel – say, your website – then they're going to think you've spun up some dodgy storefront, and behind the scenes all manner of anarchy is occurring with their cash and data. Add in a Twitter feed, a YouTube channel and a book, and – *voilà!* Instant cred.

Obviously, you build the trust by ensuring your Marketing:**Content** is consistent and coherent – that's why your potential customers are looking around for reassurance. But it's the variety of environments that reinforces the power of that messaging.

Pick four channels and dive deep. That way lies growth.

action: create a Marketing:**Distribution** media grid

Planning ahead can be quite counterintuitive when you're launching a new business. The ability to react to stimuli and change your focus at the drop of a hat sets a startup apart from its more staid competitors. However, where you can discover and apply a measure of stability in a new business, you must. This is not to stifle creativity and leave you unable to flex when necessary – it's to provide a solid foundation to express those traits with even more confidence.

I've always viewed the Marketing:**Distribution** media grid as the reassuring, comforting necessity in a sea of uncertainty elsewhere. Regardless of what's happening in the rest of the business, you'll know that every day or every week, your marketing messaging is going out via Twitter, Facebook or LinkedIn, generating interest in what you do. What it also does is build trust in you from those who enjoy your Marketing:**Content** that you're in it for the long-haul. That's a solid base to play from.

To build a media grid, you can use a productivity app (see examples on www.growtion.co) or a spreadsheet. Lay out every single day for the next year so that each one has enough space for some detail in it. Then start with your categories of ready-made Marketing:**Content**.

When are you going to release your podcast?

When are you going to drop your videos?

When are you going to publish your blogs?

The regularity of these needs to be realistic, but frequent enough that people will look out for them and miss them if they're not there. My media grid has blogs every weekday of the year (with accompanying video), weekly podcast (on Saturdays), weekly newsletter (Sunday round-up of the week's business growth stories, plus my own views, links to the podcast, etc), weekly webinar (each Wednesday lunchtime) and a daily inspirational quote that goes out on Instagram. Each of these is plugged into the grid and is a non-negotiable. If I have to wake up early to ensure that the blog is written, then I will do so. If I have to give up a Saturday night to write the newsletter for three hours, then that's what has to happen.

Guidance by the grid is a discipline that gives you confidence in what you're doing and visibility that you're always ready, always helpful, and trust in you will pay off – because you keep showing up.

resolu**tion**

This is it – you're now 'out there' with your product and your marketing. People – those you seek to serve – are starting to build expectations around you, and those expectations need to be met for trust to flourish.

There's no getting away from it – this is a responsibility now. You can't pull it back, so be very careful about what you promise – because you have to keep your promises, each and every one.

That said, you also need to take risks – isn't that why you're here, really? Because you *have* to do this? Assuming this is the case, you need to get out there and show your target audience what you've got. Because as Hillel the Elder said, 'If I am not for myself, who will be for me? ... And if not now, when?'

How can you make sure that Marketing:**Advertising** pays off?

ELEMENT 10

Marketing:Advertising

definition

'Advertising' is what everyone used to think marketing was in its entirety. The visible direct messaging that was so obvious in its intention that it, surely, didn't work – did it?

But if it did not work, how come there was so much of it around? And how come it persists in ever-greater volume each and every year?

The answer is – guess what? It does work. Very well. And it can do so for you and your launch, if you follow certain rules.

Rule 1: Don't use offline advertising

Hefty one to kick off with.

Offline advertising includes any form of paid-for promotion that isn't online, such as posters, newspaper and magazine adverts, linear TV and radio ads, and sponsorships, among others. It is hugely expensive for what it delivers, and so offline advertising should not be used by startups in any capacity.

Why? Three reasons:

A. Its genuine ROI is incalculable.

B. It is inflexible.

C. It does not suit early-stage brands.

Take reason A; this is no surprise to you, is it? It uses the word 'incalculable' in the sense of both 'not technically able to be calculated' and 'astonishing in its reckless wastage'. The inefficiency of offline advertising is a feature, not a bug.

There was a time when offline advertising was the only way to do Marketing:**Advertising** – back then, as a startup, you had an excuse. You do not have an excuse anymore.

The inflexibility of offline advertising is also a matter of record. You can't craft an offline campaign in one morning, plug it in during the afternoon and change it the next day based on its impact. You generally have to plan it some weeks, if not months, in advance. You then have to stick with it, even if the results are terrible. Inflexibility for a launch ad campaign can leave the startup spluttering on the launch pad. In addition, you are likely to have to fit your creative messaging into set structured formats that say more about the environment that you're advertising in than you and your brand.

Finally, the relevance of offline advertising to new brands is almost zero. If you are a major multinational with a budget in the millions, you could go after a mass audience quickly using offline advertising, but building trust is a long game, and that doesn't happen with one single campaign to put your Marketing:**Brand** on the map.

Unless and until you have some brand attributes that people recognise and understand, throwing budget at a brand campaign is pointless. It should only ever be a reinforcer of what people already know about you.

Rule 2: Start small

I'm sure you have understood the rule about launch businesses and offline advertising, but you also need to be mindful of what works and what does not in online advertising.

The first thing to appreciate about online advertising is its unbeatable flexibility, but this does come with one downside. The sheer variety of locations for your campaigns means that you could potentially spend the budget many times over to reach the same people. The upside of being able to test multiple platforms and creative ideas within a tiny budget allocation is that, with a little patience and precision, you can find what works and exploit it to the max.

To do this, you need to start small. The minimum budget tends to be around £8 per day, and you'll want to run each test for at least a week to give enough of a flavour of what might and might not work. Consider these as 'micro-tests' of your theories of what is going to appeal to your audience. Recall where they hang out from Marketing:**Intel** (E07) as well as what Marketing:**Content** (E08) is already out there.

As far as being creative is concerned, you'll have what to say from your Product:**Concept** (E01), of course. You can play around with how to articulate it, drawing on the strapline (if any) you created in Marketing:**Brand** (E06). In the latter element, you'll have pulled together some images which can serve as foreground or background pieces to standardise the look and feel of the adverts that you're creating.

Every advert, of course, needs a CTA – the thing that directs the interested party in what to do next. Generally speaking, this will be the key activity that we'll spend more time on in Sales:**Activity** (E14). It is worth waiting until you've completed that element before you start a campaign in earnest, as until you know what this key activity is, the effectiveness of your micro-tests will necessarily be limited.

Rule 3: Measure ROI

Paid-for online Marketing:**Advertising** – be it via sponsored Facebook posts, Google keyword ads, LinkedIn placements or AdRoll retargeting – is measurable. It may feel quite fiddly, it may be something that you want to get someone else to help with, but the point of measuring it is that you can deal with a genuine question and a genuine answer – 'How much does it cost for me to make this work?' And once you have the answer to that, you can check it against how much each option generates in return and – *voilà*! A real picture of your ROI.

This is what makes Marketing:**Advertising** such a strong standalone element. It is not the same as Marketing:**Distribution** (E09) which, while demonstrably cheaper, does not bring with it the ability to scale directly. Throwing more social media posts out might provide visible evidence of investment, but it can't provide a linear expectation of return. It's not directly scalable.

Marketing:**Advertising** is scalable – directly, predictably and wonderfully so.

Rule 4: Adapt your strategy

A quote famously attributed to Mark Twain, 'Data is like garbage. You'd better know what you're going to do with it before you collect it' is a truth that holds here in Marketing:**Advertising**. You need to use the ROI numbers that you've collated for your campaigns to inform your next steps.

Recall that the aim of your entire business, articulated in Product:**Concept** (E01)'s answer to the question 'Why am I solving this problem?', is to serve as many people as you can who are suffering with the issue, whether they realise it or not. It is, therefore, your duty to ensure that you are not only taking readings of where your micro-tests are scoring, but also moving budget towards those that are working at the expense of those that are falling flat.

Rule 5: Know when to stop

That brings us on to the final rule in Marketing:**Advertising** – know when to stop.

Whether it's a launch campaign that has gone on for over a year or a once pitch-perfect piece of creative content that has become irrelevant due to a pandemic, you need to retire campaigns when they've served their purpose and go again. This is part and parcel of the skills you need in Marketing:**Advertising**. In general, a refresh every three months serves to reinforce your message and attract those who, for whatever reason, may not have participated in your product via previous campaigns.

GROWTH EXECUTION TIP #1008 - WHY IS OFFLINE ADVERTISING TERRIBLE FOR MY SME?

There is a temptation to widen the search - to dilute your messaging and reach out blindly for more customers, any customers, to sell them whatever you can. This will damage your SME significantly.

You need to take the opposite action. Home in on those you are here to serve more distinctly and specifically. They will understand when things are tough - who doesn't? - but if they believe that you are there to help them in the medium term, they may, if they can, help you in the short term.

It's hard out there. No SME finds attracting customers easy, but changing your whole approach - compromising your Product:**Concept** - will only alienate your current pipeline while confusing the heck out of everyone else.

There are more of your target audience out there. Go find them in groups on Facebook and LinkedIn, chatting about your hashtags on Twitter and sending pictures that resonate with your concept on Instagram. They haven't evaporated. But you need to work hard to find more of the right customer, not just more of any customer.

GROWTH EXECUTION TIP #1023 - HOW DO I USE ADVERTISING TO SCALE UP?

You are in business at the right time. Congratulations! There has never been a better time in the history of humankind to be advertising.

You can use the most refined and tailored targeting to hit the handful of people who are right in your sweet spot. Or you can go broad and splash messaging to a global audience at the click of a button.

But there is a catch - of course there is. People are used to all of the different ways that they're being targeted now, so to be effective, you have to have your messaging, your content, nailed. You have to know the people you are here to serve as well as, if not better than they know themselves.

Once you have a message, test it on small numbers first. You can do campaigns on Facebook and LinkedIn for a few pounds a day to see what works. Then scale it up - if it works for a hundred people, hitting a thousand will broadly achieve ten times the response.

Advertising is only expensive if you waste money on ineffective messaging. Test your Marketing:**Content** on a few of your target audience, iterate for success - then decide how busy you want to be.

ac**tion**: use retargeting to amplify your Marketing:**Advertising**

I'm sure you've experienced looking at a random item on a website – say, a toaster – and then you're looking at another site, perhaps reading up on some news, and you see the same toaster appear in an advert alongside the article that you're reading.

That's retargeting, the desired outcome of which should be the CTA that you have identified elsewhere – generally the key activity that we'll cover in Sales:**Activity** (E14). The work to be done here is threefold: choose a desired outcome, choose a retargeting provider, then execute on the campaign.

Quick technical summary – for anyone to see your retargeted ads, they have to have visited your site, and your site needs to have a special 'pixel' inserted into it which recognises the provider and the device that the visitor is on. This is dead easy and is explained in all the providers' instructions sections. And choosing a retargeting service is straightforward – as ever, there are examples on www.growtion.co that are updated regularly.

Executing on the campaign is then about ensuring your visuals match your branding, so that the person sees something that looks entirely familiar to them, and guiding them through to your desired outcome. Remember, they've already visited your website, so they have a reasonable idea of who you are. Even if they bounced quickly off it, the vast majority will have retained a memory of your Marketing:**Brand** (E06) and be able to associate it with the values you set out in Product:**Concept** (E01). If it's for them, repetition will encourage action.

Just like a standard Marketing:**Advertising** campaign, each retargeting campaign has to stand or fall on its results. You need to continue to monitor all results, make changes where things aren't working well enough, and know when to stop and change the campaign. Done well, retargeting will amplify your Marketing:**Advertising** campaigns and drive a higher ROI on each.

resolu**tion**

When you're designing a Marketing:**Advertising** campaign, begin with the end in mind. What is the key activity you want to drive your target audience to? Then pick your budget and start small. Iterate to a successful ROI by measuring the campaign consistently, but always be mindful of when you might need to stop.

This is an optional element. You don't have to advertise at all; you can go for launch without it, but there is no doubt that it will enhance your chances of success. And once you have established yourself somewhat, advertising can scale your business predictably and profitably when you have seen what works.

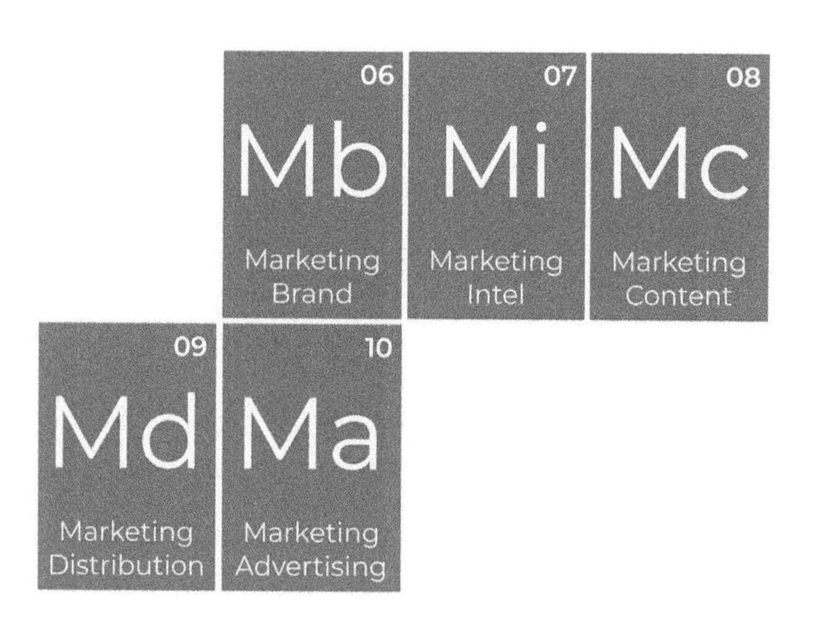
06
Mb
Marketing Brand
07
Mi
Marketing Intel
08
Mc
Marketing Content
09
Md
Marketing Distribution
10
Ma
Marketing Advertising

completion

And that's how marketing is used to launch your product. To recap quickly:

E06 – Marketing:**Brand.** This is shorthand for your Product:**Concept**. It's the first thing that people will generally see about you, so it needs to be consistent, coherent and reflective of what you are here to do. Focus on typefaces, colours, iconography, imagery and a strapline or catchphrase.

E07 – Marketing:**Intel.** You're answering a lot of data questions in this element of the Growth Execution Formula. Who are the people you're here to serve? What do they like? What are they thinking? And critically, how do you find them? The answers to these inform everything about how you approach and attract them.

E08 – Marketing:**Content.** Repurposing the same Marketing:**Content** through different media not only ensures consistency in what it says, it also saves you a significant amount of time in thinking about what to say and how to say it. Think in terms of audio, video and text, and ensure that your website provides access to all other media.

E09 – Marketing:**Distribution.** This is how you get your content out in the most cost-effective and widely distributed way possible. Google says that you need eleven touches across seven hours in four different environments, on average, for people to consider buying from you. Hit all of these notes as quickly as possible with judicious planned use of social media, PR, etc.

E10 – Marketing:**Advertising.** There are five rules to abide by in Marketing:**Advertising**: don't do offline ads; start online ads small with micro-campaigns; measure ROI; adapt your strategy when you get the success numbers back; and know when to stop. Get this right and you've got a business that you can scale predictably and well.

It's within this Marketing discipline that you need to get your MVP out. Do it. That MVP then becomes the prototype which you iterate towards PMF (see Product:**Design** [E02]). Once it's closer to a complete product, you can start to think about how you're going to operate a sales team.

It's time to have a look at that in detail. Ready?

Let's get growing.

DISCIPLINE THREE
SALES

introduction

There are three critical things to remember as you work through the five elements of the Sales discipline:

1. **Sales is the most feared discipline.** Whether you think that you like Sales or not – and the majority of entrepreneurs I know would not go on record as saying they enjoy it at all – it's the most brutal of the three disciplines.

The reason? It's unforgiving. You can play around for a long time in Product, should you choose to (don't choose to). In Marketing, you can tweak a campaign for ages without committing it to launch (don't tweak for ages). But in Sales, there's nowhere to hide. You are either selling or you are not selling. The end requires whatever means fit within your Product:**Concept** (E01), right up to the line.
You simply have to be out there, pitching, hustling, rainmaking – call it what you like, but without a concerted effort in the Sales discipline, almost all of the effort you have put into Product and Marketing will be wasted.

Asset-stripping is what happens to the lucky businesses that don't do Sales. The unlucky ones just disappear. You simply can't rely on Marketing to do the heavy lifting, nor Product to be so super-attractive that it sells itself. No – this is a serious business, and you need to embrace the fear and get your arms fully around Sales. The alternative – particularly as you're launching – is just too sad to contemplate.

2. **Win Sales and you win it all.** Back in Product:**Pricing** (E04), you thought about a thirty-six-month plan. In Sales:**Goals** (E13), you'll detail this out further. This is not simply a box-ticking exercise; the insights that this activity provides feed into what you need – and by articulating them, you transform a want into a need – and are fundamental to your success.

Once you have your plan laid down, achieving it is more than just a practical step-by-step progression to completion. It becomes emotionally involving – and that is why Sales is more than transactional. In the end, there are two humans involved in a deal and, in your business, one of those humans is always you.

That is why winning this discipline, winning Sales, is more than just a nice-to-have, a fuzzy feeling of relief mixed with satisfaction. It's everything. Building a product satisfies your past, the build-up to here. Crafting marketing campaigns satisfies your present, makes it all real. Sales is how you satisfy your future.

3. **Sales leads to scale.** The five elements of Sales – Process, Collaboration, Goals, Activity and Success –

are laid out in this section as a pathway to realising your business dreams. Once you've got there, though, where do you go?

Achieving what you set out to do is an amazing and life-affirming moment. But this handbook won't drop you there – you need to think about what's next, too. And scale is what that looks like.

Why are these two rather dull words a pair of the most important in your business's launch?

ELEMENT 11

Sales:**Process**

defini**tion**

'Sales' is a word that strikes fear into many an entrepreneur. 'Process' is an equally uncomfortable word for most. Put them together and what do you have? The least appealing element in the whole Growth Execution Formula. And yet it's one of the critical elements to understand, or you're growing nowhere.

It is almost as if the utilitarian requirement of your sales is at odds with the mysticism of product creation and the beauty of a marketing vision. In its cold, rational scanning of the horizon for those who are actually going to purchase what's on offer, the Sales discipline gives the lie to any mythmaking in Product and Marketing. But we are here to make money, people, and we need to do it well if we're to achieve the *why* we so clearly articulated in Product:**Concept** (E01).

By the way, if you still haven't completed Product:**Concept**, not only are you terrible at following instructions, you're also making life a lot harder for yourself. Go back now – go on! You can thank me for it later.

Mastery of Sales:**Process** is critical to the success of your launch. The product that you've expended so much energy in crafting; the marketing that you've so lovingly created around it; all is at risk because of a prejudice against the oldest transfer in town – the two-way benefit exchange.

Let's now take a high-level look at the distinct feature of Sales:**Process**, the sales funnel. This is not an element to swerve, no matter how tempting it is to believe that you can simply 'build it and they will come'. That belief is where, and why, most of the idealistic entrepreneurs wind up with nothing. Don't be that entrepreneur.

The sales funnel

Sales:**Process** is all about the funnel. You will have received leads from your excellent work in the Marketing discipline, so you need to ensure that they are nurtured through to success in the most effective way possible. These leads will drop into the top of a notional wide-lipped funnel. Your job in Sales:**Process** is to get almost every one of them from the top all the way out of the bottom as the committed, delighted and noisily paying customers you want them to be.

Every business's sales funnel is different, but they all share four common features:

- Interest
- Engagement
- Conversion
- Commitment

Let's look at each of them in turn.

Interest. Your marketing campaign is awesome. It is driving leads through to the sales function and you're ready with funnel opened wide. But already, some risk is entering your Sales:**Process**. Where do these leads go? Who deals with them? How are they driven to the next funnel stage?

This is a classic area that catches out new business owners. Giving in to the temptation to leave this to chance, to assume that you'll be able to work it out when it happens, is one of the most irresponsible things that you can do with your nascent organisation.

These first leads – the potential early adopters – are the people who are going to tell the others who come after them just how great you are. That magnifying effect – the social proof from those who choose to go first – is absolutely critical to your early, and then sustained, success.

You cannot allow the process – the Sales:**Process** – from interest to engagement to become randomised. Your first job is to get the lead interested. That means working out when you are initially going to communicate with them, when you are going to follow that up if they don't respond and how many times you're going to keep hitting them before you give up.

This is the first part of Sales:**Process**. Every time that you fail to capture and convert an identified lead into an engaged prospect, you're damaging the business exponentially further down the line.

Practical ways to succeed in this are to drive leads to an online demo, offer them a 'free gift' that they have to claim directly and/or partner with someone who you can bundle interest, and therefore sales, in with. We'll explore option three in much more depth in the next element, Sales:**Collaboration** (E12).

Engagement. Inevitably, there will be one key activity which, when undertaken by the prospective customer, has the highest chance of converting them through to a successful sale. This is the activity that every piece of marketing should be warming leads up for as a CTA; it's the engagement that moves the client further forward on to conversion.

You will, however, need more than one way to engage your interested party. Some people respond well to visual media, so sending them a personalised video – even if it's a 'Hello, Jane!' message you're holding up in an image that you then use for every Jane in your prospect list – has a great track record of attracting engagement.

Others listen to audio in the car, in the shower, when they're running. If you feature on a podcast – or create your own – it can be really impactful in terms of building trust in your expertise, which is the main component of successful sales, particularly from a distance.

Finally, old-fashioned text – such as that which you're reading right now – has immense power to get people engaged with your marketing message and, ultimately, your product through sales.

Conversion. This is when the prospect says yes. You've done the hard work, got them where you want them, pitched the solution to their problem and they've gone for it. It's a great moment – but it's critical to observe that this isn't the successful endpoint of the funnel.

People say that they'll buy things with genuine sincerity, but then leave you holding on for any number of super-frustrating reasons. Things change – pandemics hit, certainties erode, lethargy sets in. Conversion isn't commitment; they are two entirely separate things, which is why you need your prospects not only to say yes, but also to prove it.

Commitment. This is the big one – when the prospect signs on the line and a new customer is inducted into your business. It's only once they cross this threshold that they become a bona fide client. Until then, they're still in the funnel and you have to find ways to nudge them further down at every opportunity.

As prospects travel through each level of the funnel, there will be inevitable 'leakage' as some simply drop out. Your first job is to measure this – of every 100 leads who come into the top of the funnel, how many on average don't get past interest? How many stick in engagement? What's stopping them from moving through conversion into commitment? Measuring these is one thing – doing something to improve them is quite another.

It is critical to understand how – and why – your Sales:**Process** funnel behaves the way that it does, so that you can widen each stage for more and more prospects to drop through. Every percentage point that you can increase the numbers falling through a level of the funnel is a huge multiplier of profit on your bottom-line.

GROWTH EXECUTION TIP #1101 - WHERE DO I START WITH SALES?

Sales is important. Your product - no matter how much you would want this to be true - is not going to sell itself in enough quantities to grow your business as fast as you need. Therefore, you need to get a grasp of sales.

The first thing to do is to understand your Sales:**Process**. Your future customers need to move from interest, through engagement and conversion to commitment. At each of these levels of the sales funnel, some will fall out. Your job is to understand why and minimise this leakage.

The tools that you use to move prospects through your funnel will be critical to the success (or otherwise) of your venture. Identify the key steps that you need to usher your targets through this process now - then iterate as you become more mindful of what works and what does not.

Sales is going to get harder in the coming months. You need to start practising now.

GROWTH EXECUTION TIP #1107 - PUTTING THE FUN INTO YOUR PROFIT FUNNEL

The sales funnel has received a lot of interest in recent years, as it has become ever more straightforward to identify and track individual prospects through from interest to commitment.

In any business, this activity is critical to profitability and success. The more clients you can capture the attention of through marketing who then convert via your structured Sales:**Process**, the more you make from them not only once individually, but also multiple times from the identification and implementation of a repeatable system.

To build a funnel, I always look at four areas: interest, engagement, conversion and commitment. Assume that your marketing is working hard enough for interest to be coming. Engagement can occur through the customer's registration with you. This can then drive drip campaigns, identifying those who interact with more of your output.

Conversion is when the prospect agrees to buy. This can be when they put something into their basket online or sign a contract, but until they've paid, the final stage - commitment - hasn't occurred and you're still not in profit.

Break your Sales:**Process** into these four areas and identify one thing that will increase the throughput of each. All will have an eye-opening impact on your profits at a stroke.

action: plug your leaky Sales:Process funnel

This is where it can get dispiriting. You've worked so hard to get the product up and running, to get the marketing plans delivering leads, but your target customers, stubbornly and rudely, do not end up buying from you. What on earth is going wrong?

At each stage, where people are not progressing, you have to open a GAIT. This stands for:

- Gather
- Assume
- Iterate
- Test

Gather. Use a customer relationship management (CRM) system to monitor volumes. See where things are leaking and select the worst leak first – the higher up the funnel, towards the entry-point, the more prospects there will be with the potential to drop through to other areas.

Assume. You can try asking those who don't drop into the next funnel level why this is, but you're unlikely to get much feedback – these people have often already checked out. Instead, make some reasoned assumptions on what's going wrong and consider the most likely.

Iterate. Just like when you iterated your Product:**Design** (E02) from a lump of stone into a beautiful sculpture, you're finessing the funnel at this point. Once you have your assumptions crystallised, pick one easily implementable high-impact change and mark the moment that you put it into action, so that you can clearly define cause and effect.

Test. Here, you're testing the amended funnel with more of the leads coming in from your marketing. It's really important to remember that the majority of your funnel activity will be around making improvements to fix leaks. This stage is critical – and you must ensure that the change doesn't cause an imbalance anywhere else in the funnel.

These four steps, repeated multiple times at each leaky level of your Sales:**Process** funnel, will help to stop leaks and ensure a higher percentage of prospects going all the way to commitment at the bottom.

resolu**tion**

Sales:**Process** is the first and most important of the Sales elements. It's where the planning takes place to ensure that the rest of the efforts you deploy through the discipline aren't wasted.

Take time to define each stage of your funnel and assess the throughput of leads coming into it from marketing. Once you have an understanding of the main leaks, open a GAIT repeatedly to improve each issue.

Working this element hard early postlaunch will give you insights into your Sales issues and maximise the returns on the efforts that you're putting in now, as well as those that are to come.

Who's talking to your customers already?
Partner-up and grow faster.

ELEMENT 12

Sales:Collaboration

definition

As a species, it's fair to say, we humans have punched above our weight. The very fact that you're reading these words is testament to your ability to decode collections of contrived symbols into a shared meaning, and for that meaning to then be repurposed to further your own ends.

Collaboration is what enabled early humans to win together over time, sharing knowledge about risks and opportunities available in the next wild valley and providing our ancestors with the critical survival instinct that has made its way down to us here, today.

It's probably also fair to say that those who did not share this collaborative instinct were more likely to perish in interesting and, in all probability, lonely ways. In short, humans fare better when we collaborate. And that is true of humans in the business arena as well as those on the savannah floor.

Why does something so self-evident warrant its own element? With only five available in Sales, can collaboration really justify 20% of your sales attention?

Yes. And the reasons are both strategic and tactical. However, before we get stuck into those, there is one overriding question that I always get asked whenever I posit the idea of a new startup partnering with an established company:

'What if they steal my idea?'

This is *such* a prevalent fear that it deserves to be addressed head on. First of all, yes, of course you need some sense around this. If you approach the biggest player in the market and dangle the best idea that they've yet to notice in front of them, you have a rational fear of creating a problem. That said, the chances are that they'd have got around to doing it already if they thought it was that good – they will have people paid handsomely to think of this stuff.

In general, though, at this early stage, it's wise to avoid the 'big beasts' in your actual or adjacent markets. They will be unlikely to encourage you and likely – if it is a good idea – to find ways to obstruct your progress.

What you're really looking for is a business that's a couple of years ahead of yours in a complementary adjacent market – one which, critically, deals with the clients that you're targeting. Paying close attention in Marketing:**Intel** (E07) will have shown you other businesses that are already playing in this space. Assuming it's a normal industry – not one that is involved in clandestine corporate operations or international governmental espionage – you'll find a few businesses that are like yours but have been around a little longer.

Carry that close attention on into examining their ethics and business models. Here, yet again, is evidence of the importance of getting your Product:**Concept** (E01) articulated correctly at the start of your business creation. You can deploy it externally as well, to check that your potential partners live up to your ideals and will help you to get closer to where you need to go – or not.

These businesses will not be interested in copying your idea. They will be two years into a three- or five-year plan and not looking to rip you off. Get a non-disclosure agreement (NDA) in place to help you sleep at night, then get ready for the good stuff.

Credibility

This is what you get from a great Sales:**Collaboration**.

We spoke in Marketing:**Content** (E08) about trust and how to establish it. Trust is the one thing that every customer needs to have a modicum of in you if they're going to buy from you. By partnering with an organisation that has already proven itself so trustworthy to enough of your future audience that it's got them paying, you're shortcutting the trust-build phase and borrowing credibility from them.

Be mindful that this cuts both ways, which is why you have to be so careful when selecting the right partner. As in a marriage, you'll still be associated in many people's eyes with this organisation long after you've split. If you're an ethical business partnering with one that sources products from child labour camps, you're likely to find yourself with some awkward customer questions to answer in your live chat in due course.

From the position that you are in, launch, being able to articulate your vision and persuade a credible partner to link arms with you is a huge step-change in your own visibility and integrity within the market. Always be looking out for these opportunities as they will skip you forwards a year or two in growth, if used correctly.

Data

This is the thing that, on the face of it, has the most direct value from a collaboration. As partner of a credible business that's already speaking to the audience you seek to serve, you will have access to these customers of theirs, too. Being able to cross-promote your Marketing:**Brand** (E06) and product to these people in tandem with ones they recognise already will lead to more sales, without a doubt. The database that your partner has launched you out to will respond and become part of yours.

You would never have reached this number of people without the partner's help. And because you know that the customer is into the partner, they're going to be into you, too – particularly when the partner is the one emailing them, talking about you on videos and/or integrating you into their customer-facing systems.

Advice

This is the one that can be easily missed when you're looking to maximise the value that comes from Sales:**Collaboration**. Your partner has already been where you are, trying to talk to these people and get their business.

To shortcut many of the issues that you're inevitably going to face, why not keep a strategic conversation going with your partner as you work together to complete the deployment of the partnership? There may come a time when they stop talking to you about things that are not directly partnership-related, but – if that moment does come – perhaps they're showing their colours a bit and you might want to question how much deeper you want to go with them.

Sales:**Collaboration** is a contact sport. Now that they're visibly partnering with you, it becomes in your partner's interests for you to thrive, too. This is one of the keys to leveraging a great partnership – get the advice you need to make you stronger, as well as the borrowed credibility and data that will come as standard.

Humility

One final piece of advice before we move into the Growth Execution Tips and the ac**tion** for this element, Sales:**Collaboration**: be humble.

It is tremendously easy, particularly when you have secured a deal with a larger organisation and are as excitable as a kid in a toyshop with your new project, to be cocky. I have seen great potential partnerships collapse, to the detriment of both sides, simply because the junior partner is throwing their weight around and demanding things that the senior partner either can't or won't do in the timeframes that the upstart startup wants.

Humility. This is an overlooked skill in the human repertoire these days. When everyone seems to be getting their own way by shouting very loudly, actually getting on and doing what you agreed you would, letting your partner complete their responsibilities in their own good time, is where great Sales:**Collaborations** are forged.

GROWTH EXECUTION TIP #1202 – SHORTCUT THE WAY TO YOUR AUDIENCE

Creating a partnership with a non-competing organisation in your space gifts you three things:

1. **Borrowed integrity and credibility.** The 'halo effect' of being seen in the company of partners already trusted by your target audience can't be overstated. Yours suddenly becomes an organisation that is worth doing business with.

2. **Access to an audience that you would otherwise spend years building.** One shared Tweet or standalone email shot to your partner's base and you've hit a tailored marketplace of targets at a stroke.

3. **Advice and guidance on how to succeed.** This is the one that is most commonly missed, usually because new partners forget to ask for it. Now that you are working together with your partner, it is absolutely in both your interests for your business to succeed, so ask what has made them so successful. How have they navigated this pitfall or that one? What's the best advice they can give? Which customers are the ones that will help the partnership to grow the fastest?

Look around now at the other organisations operating in your space and reach out to three today. If you're already working with some, go find some more.

Sales:**Collaboration** is a critical means of growth execution and it requires your urgent attention, right now.

GROWTH EXECUTION TIP #1208 – WHAT'S THE MOST IMPORTANT THING TO LOOK FOR IN A POTENTIAL PARTNER?

To grow quickly, you will want to find other businesses that are already talking with your ideal customers. By being associated with them, you can fast track your brand into the minds of those that you seek to serve, 'borrowing' credibility from the years your partner has spent building theirs up and super-charging your growth.

But be warned – there are dangers lurking here, too.

If you don't understand what the partner's Product:**Concept** is – why they are doing what they are doing – you may find that, for their own perfectly logical reasons, they veer significantly away from their current path. You could be swept along into a place where you are associated with a business that screams its support for a political movement that disgusts you or has a stance on the environment that completely conflicts with your own ethical position.

Always discover what a potential partner's Product:**Concept** is. Ask them, 'Why?' Why are they doing what they're doing, solving the problem that they're solving?

It's a question that we should all continually be asking ourselves, of course, and anyone who is going to be sharing a platform with our Marketing:**Brand**. Otherwise, we could be hitching our precious cart to a horse that could end up charging anywhere...

action: build a true Sales:**Collaboration**

We've spoken already about how to find the right partner – a company a couple of years ahead of yours in an adjacent industry with the same outlook as yours. But what happens when you have found them?

How do you talk about the partnership itself? What do you look out for? How do you know it's going well and what happens if it fails?

The first thing to decide is whether you want what we'll call a 'soft' or 'hard' integration.

Soft integration. This can be as simple as both you and your partner publishing a press release stating that you are now in partnership. Both CEOs commend the other and it appears in some industry websites as fact.

You can also offer a discount to those who are provided with a code from your partner to add a bit more urgency and utility to the collaboration, as far as the consumer is concerned.

Hard integration. This is where data swaps are automated, consumer experience is seamless between the two organisations and meetings are held regularly between representatives of both to discuss shared objectives and overcome any issues. In all honesty, this kind of partnership is likely to happen some time after your launch – and that's to be appreciated. You need to prove each partnership works before you get sucked into spending too much time on it.

Broadly speaking, the softer and quicker the integration at this stage, the better for you. You get all of the credibility and advice uplift with much of the data, too, without having to create a whole huge operational facility to leverage the right outcomes from the partnership.

A final word of warning to end this element's ac**tion** section – be prepared for problems. Anything bespoke – which almost every partnership is by definition – is going to require patience, perseverance and flexibility to overcome what will seem like existential issues every once in a while.

When these issues arise, stay calm – if you can prove to be the partner who doesn't get fazed by issues, you're going to be the one that your collaborator keeps looking to build and grow future communications around. This is an opportunity for you to supercharge your business using someone else's costly built network.

Make it count.

resolu**tion**

There are so many good reasons to develop an ecosystem of great partners that any concerns you might have about your idea being ripped-off should take a far-back seat to the benefits on offer. Yes, you need to make sure that there's an NDA; yes, you need to avoid the biggest sharks in the tank; but broadly speaking, I have never come across any business owner who has truly regretted working with another business that's similar to theirs, but just a bit ahead.

In time, of course, even more exciting opportunities will arise to leverage your relationships with these organisations. Who knows? One of them might be so impressed with what they know of you and your business that they consider an acquisition.

That's for the future, though. For now, as you're starting to get some serious visibility with the right kind of partners, let's look at where you want to take it.

It's time to get structured in Sales:**Goals**.

What targets should you set and over what period do you chase them down?

ELEMENT 13

Sales:**Goals**

defini**tion**

Some people are driven by Sales:**Goals** and targets – others, less so. One of the things that I've observed in hundreds of entrepreneurs I've spoken with over the years is that, particularly early on, they're rarely working towards a definitive number in three years' time.

It's evident to me that those who do are the more successful by far.

That's why this is such an important element. It's not one that most clients really enjoy, but it is one that ends with them having a clear direction and destination. Those are things that – like Product:**Concept** (E01) and Marketing:**Brand** (E06) – keep giving back over time.

Once you know your direction and destination, you stop having to make decisions about them every month. You recognise what the desired outcome is, what the steps are to get there, and – if you're falling behind – you know how to analyse whether it's a revenue issue or a cost issue, which provides the context for the tough questions you have to ask to get back on track.

There are also the serendipitous moments that can help propel you towards your Sales:**Goals**, provided you know what they are. Seneca, the Roman philosopher, said, 'If one does not know to which port one is sailing, no wind is favourable,' and that goes for you and your targets, too. You can't see opportunities to get you closer to a goal if you don't know what that goal looks like.

This handbook is intended to help you launch your business and build it to a position of strength. To do that, you are going to need to do some really tough things – if this was easy, everyone would be doing it. But they're not and you are, so let's get realistic about how this needs to pan out.

What does success look like?

Far too many SME businesses fail and – I would argue – one of the main reasons is that they flail around with a product that's nice, a marketing team that's on it, but no direction from the CEO on exactly what success looks like. This is not a fate that need befall you. Remove it from the picture by understanding clearly what it takes to get to good – and then to great. It's much more straightforward to take others with you when they know where you're going, too.

Where do you start with Sales:**Goals**? First stop is a throw-forward to Month Thirty-six. Whenever today is, add three years, close your eyes and take a breath – where are you going to be?

Start with the dream. Rather than a specific amount of money that you need to achieve – which is abstract – visualise what you would be doing with that money. Would you be living somewhere completely different? Committed to an extra day off a week or month off a year?

Sustaining your drive on the back of things that you wish to do for others via your Product:**Concept** (E01) is great. If you can fold into that something that will also make an obvious positive physical difference in your life, then there is even more chance that you're going to get it done.

Then you look at what and how much you will need to get there. What's the extra mortgage going to be roughly? Or do you need to recruit someone senior in Year Two to take more of an active role in the business so that you can genuinely enjoy time away from it on those holidays? Whatever it is, you'll start to pull forward a number, one that is going to make a difference to you.

For the ease of an example, let's say that it's £20k per month in profit. You can see a basic example of how a business might get to £20k profit in Month Thirty-six in the ac**tion** section.

Now £20k is no longer just a number that will hopefully appear on a spreadsheet when the time is right. It's freedom. It's the life you want to lead. It's comfort, joy, pride in a job well done; it's what you tell your significant other when you have to work late again; it's what you tell yourself when it feels like it's getting too much.

That Month Thirty-six amount needs to live with you. And once it does, you'll fight harder than you thought possible to make it happen.

That's the beauty of Sales:**Goals**, and that's why this element deserves your time. It's not rocket science and your goal doesn't have to be perfect – what it does have to be is real and relevant to you.

There are some important dependencies within Sales:**Goals** that need a reference here, too, so that they're not forgotten when you're planning ahead. One of the critical ones is the number of units sold. We're in the Sales discipline and are about to head into Sales:**Activity** (E14) where we talk in detail about the tasks to be completed to achieve Sales:**Success** (E15). The thing you need to make sure to include here is how to incentivise a sales team to hit your set Sales:**Goals**.

First of all, it's worth recognising that there is a particular skill involved in sales. As with designing and marketing your product, professionals do it best. The best salespeople I have ever recruited have a blend of curiosity and resilience that is unusual in the rest of the population.

In terms of rewards, as a startup, you want to have as little basic salary as you can get away with and the highest performance-based on-target earnings (OTE) bonus of up to 100% of basic. If you need to attract an absolute killer salesperson who loves what you do, consider equity or share options to land them, without committing too much of your limited budget to the salary element that they get regardless of performance. That way lies high risk, over-control and resentment if things aren't working quickly – and there is no guarantee, of course, that they will.

Sharing the risk is sensible, if you can find someone who believes what you do and will gun hard for it. That – and I know I'm repeating myself here – is why it's so important to have your authentic Product:**Concept** (E01) nailed and out in the world, acting as a beacon for like-minded trench-dwellers.

The flipside of that is the requirement to have rewards that scale upwards with the manner of achievement. First of all, you need to make sure that the targets you set are significantly higher than those you really want in your thirty-six-month plan.

Hide the real numbers, for no other reason than they will confuse your salespeople. You need them always aiming above the target, because if they're only hitting 75%, you still want to be secure.

From the bottom-up, I'd never pay a bonus on less than 75% achievement. Recall that you need to get to the Month Thirty-six number and each miss is more than just numerical – it's psychological, too. It starts a reaction in the sales team where they consider the targets too high – always too high. By brute-forcing a £0 bonus at less than 75%, you're going to make people work exceptionally hard to get to that number.

From 75% to 89%, I'd pay 50% of on-target earnings (OTE), so that your salespeople go hard when they're at 85% to get to 90%. Then pay 75% OTE on 90% to 94%, 90% on 95% to 99%, 100% on 100%, then increase it in line from there (so pay 140% of OTE on 140% of target).

One word of warning, though – never, ever, cap a bonus for a salesperson. This is an act of extraordinary harm to your business, but it happens so often, I can only put it down to an emotional jealous reaction to someone's earnings. This then takes precedence over a clear economic reason to back away and let them earn whatever they can. It is not smart business – it's petty and business-limiting.

If your salespeople are winning, your business is winning. Momentum is a huge advantage early in a business's life. Providing you've done your calculations right and every sale is putting net profit into your business, then let your salespeople crack on and get out of the way.

GROWTH EXECUTION TIP #1318 – HOW DO I GET MY TEAM TO SELL?

It's really simple, many business owners think – hire the 'rainmaker' salesperson and the rest happens by magic.

I've been in businesses where these people have come in and changed the game. But do you know what they all did? They had a Sales:**Process**. They were scientists of human behaviour in the particular environment that they chose to put their prospects in, and they made the rain (revenue) come via a set structure.

The first thing that you're looking for is someone who has a process and can talk to you about conversion rates down each step of the funnel. What you're then looking for is someone who's hungry. If the current economic climate means many great talents have – for whatever reason – become available, that can benefit your business; but it also causes a problem as you have to sift through the inappropriate ones to find the one that you really need.

Present your incentive scheme and see their response. If they take it, they're right. If they want to spend too long haggling – although do remember that a bit of haggling is actually quite fun and important, as they are salespeople in the end – then cross them off the list.

This role is too crucial to work with people who don't understand the importance of Sales:**Process**, or simply don't need it enough.

GROWTH EXECUTION TIP #1301 – WHY ARE SALES GOALS IMPORTANT?

Where do you start? There's just so much to do. And the longer time goes on, the harder it becomes to take that first deliberate step into the 'new'.

Whether you're re-energising your business after a lull, or wanting to dive into something fresh after a fundamental change in your circumstances, you need to think about where you want to be. Starting without Sales:**Goals** exacerbates the fear and results in multiple stop-starts, draining more time and ultimately making failure more likely.

Take time now – you may not get it again – to work out what the next one, three, six and twelve months will look like. Think about the number of customers you want to have and the revenue that will come from them. Then do twenty-four months, then thirty-six.

Scaling the horizon gives you real perspective on what your new working life is going to look like. Then you can decide to crack on – or, if it doesn't look tempting after all, decide to do something else. But don't drift.

Without Sales:**Goals**, you're never going to be as efficient as you could be. And that means others might just get to your destination first.

action: create your thirty-six-month Sales:Goals plan

From a standing start today, £0 in Month One, we need to generate net £20,000+ by Month Thirty-six. The table shows how that might come together, giving a basic view of what a plan might look like to achieve this. Clearly, it makes some heroic assumptions regarding costs and salaries, but you'll have to give these things consideration in your own world, too.

The key variables here are the 'Units' and 'Average unit price' that make up the total revenue, and the 'Team', 'Average salary' and 'Other costs' that make up total costs. Space precludes any deep dive into all the variables, so these are necessarily rudimentary, but the guidance is here purely to give you a high-level understanding of how to build a thirty-six-month plan from scratch. If you need any further assistance, do get in touch on the Growth Execution Group on Facebook.

This particular example has a compound growth rate of 20% per month – that means that in each month, 20% more units are sold than the month before. This is clearly dependent on marketing as well as sales, so costs may have to increase over time to get your message out there.

Month	Units	Ave Unit Price	Revenue	Team
M01	0	£79	£0	1
M02	0	£79	£0	1
M03	1	£79	£79	1
M04	1	£79	£95	1
M05	1	£79	£114	1
M06	2	£79	£137	1
M07	2	£79	£164	1
M08	2	£79	£197	1
M09	3	£79	£236	1
M10	4	£79	£283	1
M11	4	£79	£340	1
M12	5	£79	£408	1
M13	6	£79	£489	2
M14	7	£79	£587	2
M15	9	£79	£704	2
M16	11	£79	£845	2
M17	13	£79	£1,014	2
M18	15	£79	£1,217	2
M19	18	£79	£1,461	2
M20	22	£79	£1,753	2
M21	27	£79	£2,103	2
M22	32	£79	£2,524	2
M23	38	£79	£3,029	2
M24	46	£79	£3,634	2
M25	55	£79	£4,361	3
M26	66	£79	£5,234	3
M27	79	£79	£6,280	3
M28	95	£79	£7,536	3
M29	114	£79	£9,044	3
M30	137	£79	£10,852	3
M31	165	£79	£13,023	3
M32	198	£79	£15,627	3
M33	237	£79	£18,753	3
M34	285	£79	£22,503	3
M35	342	£79	£27,004	3
M36	410	£79	£32,405	3

Ave Salary	Other costs	Costs	Profit	Total Burn
£3,000	£600	£3,600	-£3,600	-£3,600
£3,000	£600	£3,600	-£3,600	-£7,200
£3,000	£600	£3,600	-£3,521	-£10,721
£3,000	£600	£3,600	-£3,505	-£14,226
£3,000	£600	£3,600	-£3,486	-£17,712
£3,000	£600	£3,600	-£3,463	-£21,176
£3,000	£600	£3,600	-£3,436	-£24,612
£3,000	£600	£3,600	-£3,403	-£28,016
£3,000	£600	£3,600	-£3,364	-£31,380
£3,000	£600	£3,600	-£3,317	-£34,697
£3,000	£600	£3,600	-£3,260	-£37,957
£3,000	£600	£3,600	-£3,192	-£41,149
£2,500	£1,200	£6,200	-£5,711	-£46,860
£2,500	£1,200	£6,200	-£5,613	-£52,473
£2,500	£1,200	£6,200	-£5,496	-£57,969
£2,500	£1,200	£6,200	-£5,355	-£63,324
£2,500	£1,200	£6,200	-£5,186	-£68,509
£2,500	£1,200	£6,200	-£4,983	-£73,492
£2,500	£1,200	£6,200	-£4,739	-£78,231
£2,500	£1,200	£6,200	-£4,447	-£82,679
£2,500	£1,200	£6,200	-£4,097	-£86,776
£2,500	£1,200	£6,200	-£3,676	-£90,452
£2,500	£1,200	£6,200	-£3,171	-£93,623
£2,500	£1,200	£6,200	-£2,566	-£96,189
£2,500	£1,200	£8,700	-£4,339	-£100,527
£2,500	£1,200	£8,700	-£3,466	-£103,994
£2,500	£1,200	£8,700	-£2,420	-£106,413
£2,500	£1,200	£8,700	-£1,164	-£107,577
£2,500	£1,200	£8,700	£344	-£107,234
£2,500	£1,200	£8,700	£2,152	-£105,081
£2,500	£1,200	£8,700	£4,323	-£100,759
£2,500	£1,200	£8,700	£6,927	-£93,831
£2,500	£1,200	£8,700	£10,053	-£83,779
£2,500	£1,200	£8,700	£13,803	-£69,975
£2,500	£1,200	£8,700	£18,304	-£51,671
£2,500	£1,200	£8,700	£23,705	-£27,967

Salaries are showing that the first employee, possibly you, receives £3,000 per month, the second £2,000 and the third £2,500. Overall, month-on-month breakeven is reached in Month Twenty-nine – two and a half years into the venture. This is not unusual but is perhaps something that many entrepreneurs prefer not to think about too much at the outset. It's another reason why I'd like you to think about it here.

You need to know that you can afford this. Often, I'm struck by a clear picture that it's not the product, the marketing or the sales that a founder is going to have trouble getting to work, it's the mismatched expectation of success alongside the startup capital they require to get to month-on-month breakeven.

So many businesses die, not because their product is bad, not because their marketing is bad and not because their sales is bad – but because their owner runs out of money before achieving profitability, spending more than their capital can possibly allow. Do not let this be your fate.

Once you're there, the business essentially 'washes its face' and you can be confident that whatever startup capital you've used can be repaid in the end, all other things being equal. You can also be reasonably sure that – provided it's not entirely 'you' that is the product – there is some value in the business that you may be able to realise over time if you chose to sell it.

But that's getting ahead of ourselves. Note the value in 'Total burn' in Month Twenty-eight – that is the maximum amount this business will have lost before it starts to come down a profits flow from Month Twenty-nine.

Do you have the appetite for that? This is not a trivial question. Think on.

resolu**tion**

Sales:**Goals** is one of the hardest elements of the Growth Execution Formula. It requires foresight, brutal self-reflection and a little bit of dreaming, too. There's no getting away from it – a business needs direction. Without it, you can sleepwalk into oblivion.

We're back out into the customer-facing sales fun next, as we finally find ourselves in Sales:**Activity**. It may be the penultimate element, but it's well worth the wait.

How do you maximise the outputs from the inputs?

ELEMENT 14

Sales:**Activity**

defini**tion**

And so, it comes to this. Thirteen elements have been and gone in the Growth Execution Formula and we're finally getting active.

Of course, you've done a lot: built and iterated a Product:**Design** (E02); created a Marketing:**Brand** (E06); and got your Sales:**Process** (E11) ready and raring to go. What you haven't done yet is systemised the energy and measured the results of actually pitching and sealing deals.

That's why Sales:**Activity** is here – to draw together the strands of all of your previous work and bundle it into a transparent and flexible working arrangement. It measures what succeeds and builds confidence, jettisoning things that are peripheral. At launch, you don't have the time – or, frequently, the money – to waste energy on fruitless tasks. Sales:**Activity** is where you get serious about executing on your plans, generating Sales:**Success** (E15).

Let's start with a quick look back at the funnel you built in Sales:**Process** (E11). There were four specific stages there – interest, engagement, conversion and commitment. The job of work was to test each of these, understand where people were falling out and work to plug the leaks. That was all in preparation for the acceleration of pace that comes here.

What we discovered in Sales:**Process** is that there is one step a prospect takes that tends to be the most likely indicator of their propensity to purchase. This could be watching an online demo if you're running a remote service business, enjoying a tasting session if it's a restaurant or taking advantage of a market appraisal valuation of a property if your product is selling homes. Whichever step is the most transformative in terms of you transitioning a potential client to an actual client, that's your key activity.

Key activity

The key activity is what you want as many prospects as possible to go through, as it's the one that convinces most of them that yours is the product they really do want. Whatever drew them towards your Marketing:**Brand** (E06) in the first place, whatever made them pick up your Product:**Design** (E02) and turn it around in their hands, that instinct for the right thing for them is absolutely spot-on.

They're a genius. And the key activity helps them to prove, to themselves and to you, that this hyper-smartness is real. Your product is what they needed all along.

Identification of the key activity has three significant benefits:

1. It enables you to point all CTAs in all Marketing:**Advertising** (E10) and Marketing:**Distribution** (E09) towards this activity.

2. It provides a single key performance indicator (KPI) metric that you can use to measure the healthiness of your business.

3. It gives an additional contextual measure of the effectiveness of your sales team alongside bald sales numbers.

Once you have your key activity, it's imperative that the actions you put in place to drop people through the Sales:**Process** funnel into that key activity are SMART – specific, measurable, achievable, realistic and time-bound.

Specific. It's easy to keep things pretty 'fluffy' when it comes to tasks that you need performed. Is it a tasting evening, with people floating around chatting and nibbling, or is it a registration exercise with a team on hand to ask three quick questions at the door when someone's on their way out? Is a property valuation meeting a trial-by-small-talk potter around a person's home, or a checklist of core actions followed up by a sentiment survey around what the client thought of you and the process? The more specific you are about what you expect, the less time you have to spend translating vague results and/or repeating yourself.

Measurable. We'll go into more detail regarding setting up your own CRM system in the ac**tion** section shortly. What's important here is to recognise why you need one.

There are so many ways to expend energy on your business in fruitless endeavours – to be a 'busy fool' – that you simply have to have a structured way of ensuring that the work is getting done and the key activity is being attended to. How individuals within your team get to this point can be flexible – you'll be able to use a CRM to understand the success of their approaches, but as a non-negotiable, you need to absolutely know who's getting the key activities over the line.

Achievable. Can your team achieve what you're asking them to do? Do they have the tools at their disposal? Have they been trained appropriately? Are there enough hours in the day?

Anyone who's run a sales team will know the creativity that can go into excuses why numbers haven't been hit – and the 'unfair targets' is a major one. Cover it.

Realistic. This one's a judgement call. Essentially, you have to put in place a number that you think is doable. The best way – but not the only way – to head-off arguments that this number is a terrible over-statement of capacity is to have demonstrably achieved it yourself in the past.

Again, this is where having a CRM system that shows categorically what you've managed to achieve in a few days of executing on the key activity can go a long way towards heading-off future complaints. It also shows that you know exactly what's required and you're not afraid to roll your sleeves up.

Time-bound. It's all very well knowing the volume of key activities that need to be completed, but without a deadline, you'll lose out in the long run. In Sales:**Goals** (E13), you set some pretty strong timeframes for your personal idea of what Sales:**Success** (E15) looks like. They need to be folded in here so that you can be confident your thirty-six-month plan is not going to slip.

This is a good discipline for you. Frequently, particularly in businesses that are in danger of failure when events arise to challenge their core mechanics,

I find adherence to timeframes is viewed as optional rather than mandatory. The more strongly you hold to these timescales yourself, the more your team and the wider business will, too.

Inputs = outputs

There is no doubt that the more effort you put into anything, the more chance you have of achieving what you set out to do – that's a given. But it's the times you are able to do this when things are challenging, when it's not going as well as you'd thought it would, when results are just out of reach – that's when you need to redouble your efforts and those of the team in the pursuit of the dream.

There is no doubt that this is the sweaty end of the Growth Execution Formula. It's high-contact, high-intensity with high-reward. Make sure that you've got everything you need in place when you send your people, your product and your reputation out onto the field of play. It's going to come back with a result one way or another – and you have to be as sure as you can that it's going to be the one that you've been training all this time for.

GROWTH EXECUTION TIP #1407 - RESOURCE UP

Recruitment into a growth business is one of the hardest of many hard challenges you'll face. In simple mathematical terms, if you add one more person to a group of nine, they become 10% of the team, potentially requiring 10% of the attention and responsible for 10% of the output.

That's a huge responsibility to get right - not least because getting it wrong could easily unbalance the other 90%.

How do you give yourself the best chance of success? First of all, you've got to know what the desired output of those you bring into the team is going to be. This sounds so simple, and yet it's one of the things that is often missed. In the process to get a body in - and it always seems to be such a time-consuming, tiring process - simply finding someone who reflects a broad experience of the type you're looking for, and doesn't make a mess on the carpet, can often seem to be a win.

Starting with the knowledge of what you need them to be doing and working backwards from there gives you perspective. It makes it an objective (based on output) rather than a subjective (based on cat-friendliness) decision.

Get your three-year plan in place before you go anywhere near a recruiter. People are your most valuable resource - but they can also be your most costly one, too.

GROWTH EXECUTION TIP #1108 – WHAT IS YOUR SINGLE KEY SALES ACTIVITY?

There is, without doubt, one activity that you do in sales that produces the highest profit.

It might be a meeting. It may be an online demo. But that thing is what you need to understand and home in on – and what you need to convince your audience to get to as quickly as possible.

Forget all the other vanity metrics about visits and clicks – look hard at what the key Sales:**Activity** is and how you're getting the most prospects to that moment. This is what will dictate the success of your business – or not.

ac**tion**: set up your Sales:**Activity** CRM

There are few things that pay off as much as getting the right CRM system in and watching it drive your business automatically.

When you can see at a glance the number of key activities taking place, the conversions of these into deals, the numbers coming through as leads from marketing, the volume of interactions that your business is making with those you seek to serve, and where you need to focus to improve the Sales:**Process** (E11) – that's a good day. To get there – to make that day every day – you just need to spend a bit of time upfront ensuring that your CRM is fitted around the Sales:**Activity** that you need to do.

In particular, it's important to have two components set up:

1. **Activities.** Alongside the key activity, there will be others that get you closer to this core event. You want to be able to understand quickly who's putting the effort in and what that effort is generating in terms of progress down your Sales:**Process** funnel.

2. **Automation.** Never has it been more important – or more possible – to integrate with other systems that will automatically draw in the activities of your business or your teams. There are a number of great examples on www.growtion.co of platforms and apps that speak to each other without your ongoing intervention – ones that will provide you with incredible insights of what works in your business and what does not. Let the tech take the strain where you can and automate up.

Whichever CRM you choose – again, recommendations are on www.growtion.co – ensure that it has the capacity to capture your desired activities and integrate with other systems that you use, ones which can show email campaign openers and LinkedIn profile links, record call times and lengths, send pitch decks and emails in and out. This is not something that's a nice-to-have – it's essential to ensure that your launch hits the heights that it deserves.

A final point – make this all visible, so that everyone can see it. 'Measure it, manage it' is a cliché because it's true. What's even more true is that by publishing measurements from your CRM, you're holding yourself and your teams to account. If something is going wrong, you're in it together to fix it. If someone's not performing, it's on you as much as them from a management point of view.

Get your CRM in place upfront and you'll see huge rewards over time.

resolu**tion**

After everything that you've achieved to get here, the effort you put into this element is absolutely critical to success.

Sales:**Activity** is a constant – you need to keep on keeping on. Measure what you're doing and what's working. Ensure that the effort is going in by all of those from whom it's required and drive hard for the result that you need.

This is your investment in that price. Make it count.

What happens when it all goes right? How do you keep momentum growing?

ELEMENT 15

Sales:**Success**

defini**tion**

Here we are, then. Sales:**Success**.

It's the final stop on your journey from inspirational Product:**Concept** (E01) through thirteen other elements covering everything from your Marketing:**Brand** (E06), Product:**Pricing** (E04) and Sales:**Goals** (E13) to this, the end of your beginning. The end of your launch.

If things have gone according to plan, yours is well set to become one of the new – or relaunched – businesses that succeeds. As I said right at the start, it's not the idea that is the most important thing when you're starting out; it's the execution. If you have been able to execute on all of the elements in *The Launch Handbook*, you're going to be in great shape right now.

What's next? I'm glad you asked.

The next level

This is where everyone wants to go – to the next level. But this isn't going to happen by itself. What you (always) need to do is start preparing for it in advance.

If you're reading this straight after the other fourteen elements, great. Now's a good time to think about what's to come when you are successful. If you've dipped in and out of *The Launch Handbook* along the way, also great – this is an element you'll be able to segue into pretty quickly. I'm optimistic that you're going to need it.

The first thing to know about the next level is that it requires a different mindset to the way you think about a launch or relaunch. It's not all charging forward and pulling things along through your own efforts, plans and force of will. Now, you have something to protect.

Looking behind you as well as in front of you requires a challenge to your approach, the one that has worked up to this point. Competitors will be looking across at your table and licking their lips over your tasty lunch. Customers will be aware of their positions as early adopters and will not want to see anyone coming in later who gets a better deal than them. Staff will be seeing the growth of the business and anticipating their own financial growth for having been part of it. Shareholders, stakeholders, significant others, even you – everyone is starting to smell the waft of Sales:**Success** coming into their nostrils, and the plan – your launch plan – is going to creak as pressure is exerted onto it to produce more.

That's why you need to take a break. This is the important first step on the next-level journey. To get to this point, you are likely to have had little time to switch off and just *be*. Even if you're an exerciser, a family-enjoyer and/or a social butterfly, you will not have had *enough* time away from this creation of yours. The drain on your energy from this process will have been immense.

If you can, go and spend a night away somewhere that you like. I'd recommend doing it solo, but I know that's not always possible. When you're away, though, there needs to be 'you time' with no distractions.

This element – as much as any other – is critical to the future success of your business.

Product

Obviously, your Sales:**Success** has been built on the back of the product suite that you created in elements 01–05. As with iteration back then, you need to consider iteration here, too.

What improvements can you make? Not just for the sake of it, but ones that will really move the needle in terms of sales. Remember all that you've learned – in particular, 'Does it fit in with my Product:**Concept** (E01)?' Could there be a super-premium service that you can launch, a nascent 'platinum' that might appeal to an even more affluent audience?

Think about the parts of your product that are really popular. Can you carve those out into special add-ons to the gold, silver and bronze packages? The majority of recent video games have 'skins' and 'power-ups' that you can buy as a one-off to enhance the look of your character. These are phenomenally popular and drive huge profits. Is there anything similar that you might be able to create for your customers? A certificate? Monthly surprise package? Personalised Christmas message?

Always consider your product suite to be an escalator on which customers are forever being drawn upwards towards happily spending more money on products that continue to solve their problem delightfully.

Marketing

As you've worked through the first phase – launch – you'll have golden experience of what works and what does not in attracting the people you are here to serve into your product ecosystem. There will be some things that you've done which have worked a treat, others – that I hope you have discarded – which didn't work at all. At this second stage – scale – you get to change it up a bit.

With the confidence that comes from experience, plus some additional budget, how would you re-articulate your Product:**Concept** so that it might appeal to those within your target audience that you've yet to reach? What is a blind spot for you? What nearly worked, but might just need a bit of a tweak?

This is the time to get a bit more experimental to capture more of the attention of more of your target audience. It's when you really need to expand your reach as you seek to build on your Sales:**Success** to date.

Sales

Like the other disciplines, you're looking at this stage to review and re-tool your Sales:**Process** for the next level. You'll be segmenting leads via your CRM system and building automations in which focus on the most oft-repeated tasks to save time and ensure your team spends maximum time selling.

You'll be getting more staff in, perhaps promoting some stars from the launch phase while bringing in those with experience of running larger sales teams – people who can transfuse best practice into your ambitious sales project. Whole areas of scripting, internal communications, recruitment and incentives are up for overhaul as you've learned what works and what does not, overlaying that with fresh ideas and energy from outside.

Roadmap

Finally, your business's roadmap, with its ambitious outcomes and milestones to hit, needs an update. The opportunity here is to involve your senior team, giving them not just understanding of the direction of travel and a checklist to use along the way, but also ownership from co-authoring a strategy.

There is nothing like being part of something that they have had a hand in creating for incentivising your teams to go the extra mile to make it happen.

GROWTH EXECUTION TIP #1505 - THE SECRET TO SALES:SUCCESS

Two words that strike fear into the hearts of most SME entrepreneurs are 'sales' and 'process'. For most, the product is the passion. This is what they are here to do; it's why they set the business up in the first place. Marketing is a creative pursuit, too, so most will give it a go and have a bit of fun with the messaging. But sales? Oh, dear God, no!

These are dark arts from shady practitioners, surely? They compromise the purity and integrity of the product, the self-selling wonder that the founder has so lovingly brought forth into the world. And then we're going to compound this grubbiness by adding in a super-boring process? This is not what most SME entrepreneurs have created their businesses to do.

But hang on, though. At some stage, your early adopters are going to run out and you're going to have to get active in pursuing new customers, right?

Sales:**Process** is the secret to this – and it needs your urgent attention. It has four distinct phases that new customers move through down a narrowing funnel:

1. **Interest**. You've done most of this work in Product:**Service** (E03) and Marketing:**Intel** (E07). Who's the perfect customer? What is their avatar, where do they hang out, who do they listen to?

2. **Engagement.** Again, you're using the pre-work from other elements, in this case Product:**Concept** (E01), along with

Marketing:**Content** (E08) and Marketing:**Distribution** (E09). What do they want to hear? How often and what can you automate?

3. **Conversion.** Here, you're getting them to say yes. If you have done the other work properly, this is nowhere near as difficult as it would be if you were simply hitting them cold.

4. **Commitment**. Different to conversion, because things happen between the prospect saying yes and signing formal agreements or paying. The narrower the timeframe between the two, the less likely it is that they will change their mind.

Sales is really not that hard. Yet it's where so many business owners get squeamish and just sit and hope that the product will sell itself.

You've got a long way to go until that becomes true - if it ever will. So many great products have collapsed, or will collapse, due to their founders waiting. Don't let yours be one of them.

Devise and deploy a steady Sales:**Process** that you can iterate upon as you see what works and what does not.

And learn to love these two words - 'sales' and 'process'. Their predictability is going to help you maximise your growth in unpredictable times.

GROWTH EXECUTION TIP #1520 - HOW DO I GROW?

Ever wondered why there are so many adverts around? They're there because they work.

They will work for you, too - but you have to put the effort in first.

Whereas in Marketing:**Distribution**, you put a lot into social media, PR and other less predictable channels to get your messaging out, with Marketing:**Advertising,** you're building a structured campaign (or campaigns) that you can replicate - with replicable results, too.

Start out with the cost-effective stuff - Google Ads lets you get alongside search results for people digging for things that are just like the product you're selling. Facebook has detailed audience demographics to help you target effectively. You can also see the rough numbers of people that each grouping will hit, and it will allow you to access comprehensive results so that you can iterate to success there, too.

Finally, in the B2B world, LinkedIn is unbeatable as a way to focus in on people by their job titles, companies, interests and/or geographies.

Whichever market you're after, trial your advertising through these resources - you can do it from as little as £100 - and measure the results. You can be pretty sure that when you increase the spend tenfold, you'll get ten times the results as well. And that predictability is the reason why - day after day, year after year - you'll be seeing ads for every type of product out there. And it's why you need to embrace advertising, too, if you truly want to execute on your growth potential.

> If you want insights on advertising and predictable (and unpredictable) growth, come on over to the Growth Execution Group where a positive community of growth-focused leaders, just like you, gets together to help and support each other's businesses.

action: restructure your business for Sales:Success

When you think about what your future business is going to look like once you start to scale, the first thing that you need to address is the structure.

It would be almost unheard of not to have individuals within the business who are performing more than one role. Their job title might relate to marketing, for example, but they spend a heap of their time in customer service. Or they're supposed to be in sales but are always drawn into the meetings about product development because they speak to clients all the time and have feedback.

It's now, when you have confidence in your revenues and are looking to kick on, that you want to refine and redefine what roles you are going to need in your business. It may be that you don't want to get to this structure straight away, and that's fine. But what it shows you – and those important enough to be part of your team, when you think the time's right – is what the future looks like. Allocating roles on the basis of competency, isolating gaps in skillset that you have winged so far and preparing to recruit to fill them – these are the activities of an entrepreneur coming out of their launch phase and readying themselves for the next level.

One of the roles not to forget to interrogate fully is yours. Like everyone else in the business – and, in all probability, more so – you'll have been doing a raft of different roles. If you're to be able to scale this business properly, not only are you going to have to divest yourself of many ancillary and administrative tasks, you're also going to have to recruit your replacement for a lot of the big stuff.

Succession planning can never be started too early, in my view. Even if succession is some years away, it's only by defining the 'person spec' fully and early that you know what you're looking for – and if you happen to meet that person in two weeks' time, you can start to nurture them instantly, rather than playing catch-up later.

The final thing to look at here is how your processes are geared up. If you're like the owners of most young or refreshed businesses, 'Does it work?' has been a more important qualifying question for a procedure than 'Will it scale?' Now's the time to redress that. Something gaffer-taped together might be absolutely OK when you're servicing a few customers but will lead to dismal reviews when you're into the hundreds.

Now is the time to get thinking about your business's future growth and what it might look like for you, your people and your processes. The more prepared you are for when it does happen, the more your Sales:**Success** will be the gift that keeps on giving.

resolu**tion**

Some of the elements have been really tough – this is one for you to enjoy.

Having made it to this point, take some time to appreciate the hard yards and find somewhere to take that well-earned break. Once you dive into the next era, that of scale, you'll be glad you did.

From starting to get the right structure in place, to processes and people, Sales:**Success** is a forward-looking element that links up with how you need to progress out of the launch phase and into that of scale.

Getting here has been quite the ride. The next phase is going to be even more fun.

11
Sp
Sales
Process
12
Sc
Sales
Collaboration
13
Sg
Sales
Goals
14
Sa
Sales
Activity
15
Ss
Sales
Success

completion

That's the final discipline – Sales. Let's have a quick recap.

E11 – Sales:**Process.** In this element, you're looking to discover and systemise your sales funnel to understand what the granular steps are that take your customers from interest, through engagement and conversion before finally arriving at commitment. Widening the funnel at each of these moments will exponentially increase profit.

E12 – Sales:**Collaboration.** Who are the potential partners that already sell to your target audience? These organisations are trusted by the people that you also seek to serve, so allying with them brings considerable benefits. Principal among these benefits are borrowed credibility, highly relevant data and the kind of advice that pulls you further forwards than you would have been able to achieve quickly on your own.

E13 – Sales:**Goals.** A thirty-six-month plan isn't just a document to make you fret over target achievement – it's an important mindset-crystalliser. Once you know where you want to be in three years, you have a North Star to aim for, helping you to overcome multiple unforeseen challenges along the way.

E14 – Sales:**Activity.** This is where it gets sweaty – you need to marshal the cumulative energy of all those in your sales team into a system and structure that maximises the return on that effort. With an eye on the key activity, the one that has an outsized impact on successful sales, drive the team to achieve on their own terms, as well as those of the group and business. This is fundamental to a successful launch.

E15 – Sales:**Success.** Once you have completed all of the other fourteen elements, it's time to reflect on the significant work you've done to get you and your business here. Then it's time to look to what's next – how do you improve on what you have in all disciplines and get yourself ready for scale?

Ready?

Let's get growing.

culmination

The Launch Handbook has been written to help you successfully get your new, or refreshed, business off the ground. The strategy focuses on three distinct disciplines – Product, Marketing and Sales – as the only ones you genuinely need to be great at to ensure that your business succeeds.

Product is the most important discipline, as without it there is nothing to market or sell. It is more than just a physical entity that you can touch; it also includes services. Its five elements are **Concept**, **Design**, **Service**, **Pricing** and **USP**. By the end of this discipline, you will know why you're doing what you're doing, how to get the first MVP (market viable product) out and how to progress towards the all-important PMF (product market fit).

Marketing is the heart of your business, the emotional edge. Throughout this discipline, you learn how to build a consistent and coherent representation of your Product:**Concept**, with the ultimate aim of driving as many inbound leads as possible. The elements here are **Brand**, **Intel**, **Content**, **Distribution** and **Advertising**. It is during this discipline that you launch your MVP.

The **Sales** discipline is the one that is the most feared of the three but winning in this will mean that your business flies. Its five elements are **Process**,

Collaboration, **Goals**, **Activity** and **Success**. At the end of it, not only will you have cleared your defined sales targets, you'll be looking to the future and how to scale

There are always challenging times as an SME owner. The job that you have to do is hard – if it were not, everyone would be doing it. I hope that the guidance and focus in *The Launch Handbook* help to clear away a lot of the noise that can come with setting up and launching a product – and that, if you've followed the advice, you'll find much of the stress that can be created by your venture is relieved.

If you want to catch me and ask anything you like, do pop into the Growth Execution Group on Facebook and say hi. There are many other entrepreneurs in there just like you who'll have answers and ideas that will enrich your journey.

All that's left is for me to wish you luck in your endeavours and assert that you've already done much to ensure that your launch will be hugely successful.

So, for the final time in your launch phase, are you ready?

Let's get growing.

appreciation

This book would not have been possible without love, help and support from so many people, some of whom are mentioned below. Those that aren't – you know who you are. Thanks.

Catherine Schaefer

Sarah Turner

Sarah Ruivivar

Phil Clerkin

Stephen Willard

Shayne Warden

Colleen Amos

Marie Donaldson

Daniel Priestley

Lucy McCarraher

Mike Killen

All the contributors at the Growth Execution Group

the author

Mal McCallion is the Lead Consultant with and Founder of grow**tion**.

He has been lucky enough to be part of some great growth stories, from the launches of national brands such as Zoopla and Primelocation, to the development of dozens of SMEs and high-growth young businesses over the last thirty years. In all of them, he's been obsessed with the answer to the question: 'What makes some teams succeed – and other teams fail – at business growth?'

Distilling this experience down into three disciplines – each with five elements – Mal has created the Growth Execution Formula which plots a sustainable and profitable route to launch, then high growth.

He lives in Cambridgeshire with his sons, coaches local cricket and football teams and is a keen runner.

www.growtion.co

Lightning Source UK Ltd.
Milton Keynes UK
UKHW022223140521
383738UK00007B/313